Clutter-Free
Wealth

Clutter-Free Wealth

A GOAL-ORIENTED GUIDE TO GAINING CONTROL OF YOUR AFFLUENCE

By Liz Miller, CFA & CFP®

BOOKTIQ

DEDICATION

For Ian, Katie, and Sydney.

Your unwavering confidence inspires me daily.

ACKNOWLEDGEMENTS

I would like to thank the many people who helped make this book a reality. First and foremost I thank my family. To my children, Sydney and Katie, and to my husband, Ian, thank you for your constant support and the sacrifices you made during the time I needed to write this text. Ian, thank you for your patient readings and your honest and helpful feedback.

Michael Dowling of Wool Street Publishing, thank you for your exceptional writing and editing skills, and for your consistent commitment to seeing me through this book. Julie Trelstad and Booktiq, thank you for managing this project from conception to publication. Rorie Sherman, thank you for your experienced guidance that pushed my manuscript to the next level. Leslie Keifer, my dear friend and mentor, thank you for the inspiration and constant encouragement to write the "missing" wealth management book. Charlotte Beyer of the Institute for Private Investors, thank you for the benefit of your insights and counsel that gave me the confidence to pursue this market.

Peggy McHale and Sandi Webster, thank you for showing me that I could write this book and for sharing your wonderful contacts that made the task so much easier. Gretchen Sunderland, thanks for coaching me to achieve my goals. Mandie Lupone and Robyn Ernst, thank you for pushing me onward, reading my drafts, and asking all the right questions. Finally, I wish to thank Amy Bluestone Klein, CLU, CLTC; Danny Osborne, CPA; Sal Restifo, CPA; John Tassillo, Esq. and Lori Wolf, Esq. for generously sharing their professional expertise.

Summit Place Financial Advisors, LLC
18 Bank Street, Suite 200
Summit, NJ 07901
www.SummitPlaceFinancial.com

IMPORTANT DISCLOSURE INFORMATION
Liz Miller, CFA & CFP®, is the founder of Summit Place Financial Advisors LLC, an SEC registered investment adviser located in Summit, New Jersey. Please remember that different types of investments involve varying degrees of risk. Therefore, it should not be assumed that future performance of any specific investment, investment product, or investment strategy (including the investments and/or investment strategies referenced in this book), or any of the book's non-investment related content, will be profitable, prove successful, or be applicable to any individual's specific situation. No reader should assume this book serves as the receipt of, or a substitute for, personalized advice from Ms. Miller or Summit Place Financial Advisors, LLC, or from any other investment professional. Should a reader have any questions regarding the applicability of any portion of the book content to his/her individual situation, the reader is encouraged to consult with the professional advisors of his/her choosing.

All stories in this book are based on actual experiences and may reflect a mixture of incidents. The names and details have been changed to protect the privacy of the people involved.

A Certified Financial Planner® is a federally registered mark owned by the Certified Financial Planner Board of Standards, Inc.

Printed in the United States of America

First Hardcover Edition: 2012

Illustrations by Mara Louise Cespon

ISBN 978-0-9855684-0-5

Contents

Introduction

Financial success should bring comfort and confidence. But in recent years the skills and knowledge required to manage wealth have grown increasingly complex. Unfortunately, many wealthy investors today feel overwhelmed and stuck.

Over the past twenty years, as I've managed investments for both individuals and institutions, I've noticed two disturbing trends that led me to start my own firm and eventually write this book about my clutter-free approach to wealth management:

- The number of investment choices has exploded.
- Laws have changed so often it's difficult to plan for estates or taxes.

THE EXPLOSION OF INVESTMENT PRODUCTS

The first disturbing trend is that the investment community has become product driven, innovating new investment products at a furious pace. Every week Wall Street seems to come up with some new idea to add to investors' choices and potentially to their confusion. Basic stocks, bonds, and mutual funds get new twists. Structured investments promise more protection and better returns, but they're also difficult to understand. Derivative investments—such as an insurance contract on a bond or a contract for the future price of some commodity—promise higher returns with smaller investments, but they also entail higher risk. And alternative and private investments are showing up in more and more portfolios, adding to the clutter.

Perhaps this level of complexity wouldn't be so bad if it produced significant benefits, but let's look at the track record. In the recent economic downturn, alternative investments, structured products, derivatives, hedge funds, and many of the other complex investment vehicles failed to provide investors with either greater returns or greater protection than they had enjoyed in previous recessions. And because of the greater complexity, many investors had difficulty knowing the market value of what they owned on any given day. Today these investors are still not sure how well their positions have recovered or what steps to take next.

THE EVER-CHANGING TAX AND LEGAL ENVIRONMENT

The second disturbing trend is that personal financial matters are becoming increasingly complex because tax laws, trust and estate strategies and benefit strategies keep changing. It is almost impossible to make plans with confidence, as changing political priorities leave almost every rule in question. Many wealthy families have had to struggle along without anyone to help them navigate the different challenges that cross all the wealth specialties. A number of my clients started turning to me with questions beyond their investments:

- What's the best way to help our children buy their first house?
- How can we best fund our daughter-in-law's graduate studies?
- Does it make sense for us to start a family foundation?

These are wonderful questions, but they are not the kinds of questions clients traditionally bring to their investment managers. However, I realized that my clients had nowhere else to go for advice.

Indeed, wealth management has grown so complex that families who have attained any degree of wealth can no longer manage their own financial affairs. That may not be a big problem for the ultra-wealthy; plenty of large financial services firms are eager to meet their needs. But what about other successful individuals and families whose wealth does not quite meet the minimums required to join a multi-family office, but whose needs are every bit as complex?

Although these people engage the services of accountants, insurance agents, and trust and estate attorneys, they often must resign themselves to administering their own financial affairs. They must devote time and effort to collecting the information for these professionals and coordinating their activities. To do an adequate job, they must possess considerable knowledge about what questions to ask and which professionals to call on for various needs. For a nonprofessional, that's a high-pressure assignment with a considerable degree of risk.

THE CLUTTERED WEALTH PORTFOLIO

As a result of these two trends, I am finding that many affluent families feel their wealth portfolio is like their cluttered garage. Perhaps you have one. You sort of know what's in there, but it's such a mess that you can never find what you want when you want it. And a lot of things in that garage aren't needed at all. They are simply taking up space and making it more difficult for you to park your cars. You have told yourself many times that you really should clean out that garage, but that takes time and effort. So it stays cluttered month after month, year after year.

Has your financial success increased the complexity of your investment portfolio so that it resembles a cluttered garage? You don't need to stay stuck in the clutter, and you don't need to feel overwhelmed. This book will help you gain a much better understanding of your wealth priorities and of how each piece of your wealth plan can fit together to support them.

THE STEPS TO YOUR WEALTH PLAN

Of course, some aspects of your wealth cannot be completely simplified. But just as you can clean out the hidden corners of your garage, you can construct a wealth portfolio that is more understandable and aligned with your goals. Getting out from under the clutter is a key to enjoying your wealth.

Like so many successful people, you may need an entirely new framework for managing your personal wealth. You don't necessarily need to discard the methods that have served you well in the past, but you do need to apply them within a purposeful approach focused on core values and goals. In short, you probably need to simplify. We will clean out your clutter one step at a time until you are refreshed, confident, and in complete control:

- We will take a look at your money values as the foundation to embracing your wealth.
- We will prioritize your financial goals at each stage of your life.

- We will complete the big picture by building a net worth statement.
- We will assemble a proven and experienced professional team especially for you.
- We will address the areas of risk in your wealth.
- We will allocate your portfolio for your comfort, goals, and tax efficiency.
- We will compile a basic estate plan,
- And we will introduce a clutter-free approach to your philanthropy.

In my experience, this approach to personal financial management increases clarity, efficiency, and security. I have seen many of my clients discover renewed comfort and confidence in their wealth by adopting this approach.

Before we proceed, however, I want to emphasize that this book is not meant to offer legal, tax, or investment advice. Neither is it intended to supplant the services of your personal investment advisor, accountant, trust and estate attorney, insurance agent, and other advisors. On the contrary, one of my aims is to suggest how you might better utilize the expertise of your team of professionals. I want to give you enough information to enable you to ask the right questions and assess the answers and recommendations you receive.

A few years ago it became clear to me that many of my clients were feeling a bit overwhelmed and confused. They needed a clutter-free approach to understanding and managing their wealth that would return control to their financial lives. So I started my own firm that specializes in giving wealthy investors coordinated professional services. We work with our clients to implement a goals-oriented approach to managing and simplifying their wealth. First we help them identify the priorities in their lives and then together we arrange their portfolios and their affairs to support their lifestyle and legacy goals. In the same way I help my clients, this book can help you adopt a goals-oriented approach that will bring you the clarity and control you need and deserve.

CHAPTER 1

Cleaning Your Wealth Portfolio and Your Life

The financial industry has buried investors with innovation. At the same time, the tax and legal environments keep changing. These complexities mean that affluent families are left to navigate multiple professionals on their own.

AN OVERWHELMED COUPLE

In my first meeting with potential new clients, I typically like to find out about who they are, their journey to this point in their lives, and their experiences with investment management. I also want to learn about their personal priorities, long-term goals, and other big-picture issues.

On one occasion the potential client was eager to jump into specifics. He pulled out a spreadsheet that itemized assets of about $6 million. The columns across the page identified their ownership. The husband's name headed the first column; his wife's headed the second; and the names of several deferred compensation and retirement plans headed additional columns going right.

Down the left side of the spreadsheet he had listed about twenty to thirty investment vehicles. They included multiple insurance investments, six mutual fund company accounts, several individual stock accounts, and two IRAs. At the bottom of the page I noticed that he and his wife had six different 529 tax-deferred educational savings plans for their two children.

This couple was trying to follow the diversification advice they had received from investment counselors and the media, but they had misunderstood the concept. Instead of choosing structurally diverse investments that would respond to market conditions differently, they had chosen similar types of investments that merely had different managers. The result was lots of additional complexity but very little additional security.

In fact, their assets were in so many different pockets that they couldn't begin to wrap their brains around them. It took considerable effort just to keep this spreadsheet current, and still it gave them no ability to answer such fundamental questions as "How are we doing?" They didn't know how to gauge their performance, how to evaluate the risks in their portfolio, or how they were going to get to their goals. This couple wanted to address these issues, but they couldn't figure out where to start.

The husband said to me, "I wish someone would show me the big picture." That was a realistic request but not an easy one to grant. Although this couple had been dealing with some competent professionals regarding insurance, investments, tax planning, and so on, each of these professionals saw only a piece of the overall picture. None of them had enough clarity to develop a strategy, or even offer the best advice. Furthermore, none of these professionals had the ability to take action, even if the best course for the couple could be determined.

Unfortunately, lots of successful people find themselves in a similar predicament. Year after year they channel their savings, bonuses, and other sources of income into multiple investments. They may choose the latest hot stocks, mutual funds, insurance plans, or whatever else seems attractive at the time. Then a few years down the road, they realize they have a tangled web of investments that is long on administrative headaches and short on financial purpose.

THE MOUNTING COMPLEXITY STARTED WITH INVESTMENT CHOICES

Unfortunately, the cluttered portfolio has become even more prevalent in recent years. The emergence of 401(k) individual retirement accounts in the 1980s gave it a jumpstart. As investors scrambled to invest their savings, the mutual fund industry exploded. Employers, figuring that more is better, added to the complexity by giving their employees large menus of funds from which to choose.

In the 1990s, a greater emphasis on asset allocation led to mutual fund categories such as "large cap," "small cap," and "emerging growth." These offered more diversity and even more choices. Then came the advent of managed account programs in which professional managers would manage small pieces of a portfolio with individual securities. These programs lifted the veil of mystery on mutual fund holdings, but still offered only generic, impersonal investment options.

The growth of the Internet further added to the investment clutter. Investors could now open discount brokerage accounts and execute their own investment ideas, while continuing to pursue all of their other investment choices. The Internet also brought an explosion in free investment advice offered up by professional websites as well as amateur bloggers. TV media followed the growth of the online do-it-yourself investor by offering new programs that promised investment analysis and advice. The TV programs and online blogs may have contributed to more educated investors, but their need for viewership has led them to primarily repackage old ideas to make them look fresh and different. Each investment du jour has served only to add to many investors' haphazard, "cluttered" portfolios.

COMPENSATION PACKAGES BECAME CONFUSING

Corporate compensation, too, has become increasingly complex. As a case in point let me tell you about Rick. He has had a very successful career, and every few years we have embraced a new development in his compensation package.

In the mid-1990s, Rick's career began to really take off, and he was granted stock options that vested over an extended period of time. To determine their worth, it was necessary to know on an ongoing basis both the market value of the stock and the dates when the options could be exercised.

About five years later, while some of these stock options were still in his portfolio, Rick's employer began awarding him shares of restricted stock on an annual basis. Now he had another type of investment that required constant tracking and valuation.

After yet another three to four years, he received a customized performance package that promised to reward him in the future according to how well he and the corporation performed against various external and internal benchmarks and specified goals. But since this performance right was tied to future results, its exact value couldn't be determined for another three years, when the report card was issued.

This story is not unique. In the past fifteen years, as deferred compensation plans and investment opportunities have become increasingly complex, executives have found it more and more difficult to accurately quantify and profitably manage their wealth. Some of this complexity can't be avoided. Multi-level compensation packages are here to stay, and the executives who receive them usually can't dictate how they will be structured. Without the expertise of an advisor that can help them understand their value and potential, many employees must manage the various performance securities as best as they can.

INCOME AND ESTATE TAXES ADD TO COMPLEXITY

The U.S. tax code has been overhauled only twice in the past twenty years, and it badly needs to be simplified and updated. For example, the controversial alternative minimum tax has not been materially updated since 1993. While Congress seems to recognize the need for tax reform, the current emphasis is on increasing taxes for wealthy families, not simplifying them. The prospect of major changes to the income tax regulations injects additional uncertainty into the tax-planning process.

So much uncertainty and complexity currently surrounds estate taxes that the very idea of estate planning is scary to many people. Although the estate tax was eliminated for 2010, the IRS delayed offering specifics for so long that a number of families and accountants with 2010 estates to settle are still sorting out the details. The proliferation of complex rules and laws affecting trusts and estate planning makes it difficult for individuals to plan and act with confidence. I know several families with substantial wealth who keep procrastinating their estate planning because they find the task so overwhelming. That's a very dangerous approach.

ADMINISTRATIVE BURDENS BRING MORE HEADACHES

On top of all of this mounting complexity, wealthy individuals and families who handle their own financial affairs must shoulder significant administrative burdens. For example, consider the challenges that confront an executive who has just received a package of performance rights. What steps should she take to make sure she gains maximum benefit from this reward?

Perhaps this executive will first turn for advice to her stockbroker, who might say, "Sorry, but those assets are not with our firm, so I can't give you an opinion on them." Likewise, her accountant, tax attorney, and insurance agent also may feel this matter is outside their purview.

So she attempts to gather information from the various resources and make her own decisions. But of course, collecting data and keeping everyone informed will require quite a bit of time and effort. What's more, she will need to know what questions to ask and what information to pass on, which at times could require more knowledge than she has. There's a rather high probability that she will overlook some important matters and make some costly mistakes.

THESE COMPLEXITIES DEMAND EXPERTISE

Perhaps you accumulated your wealth through the financial developments of the past couple of decades, struggling to understand each new opportunity. Or maybe you have recently started, and you are faced with an ocean of choices. Either way, it is clear that today there are just too many investment options to consider by yourself, and too many issues to address without the benefit of professional advice.

You deserve the expertise of qualified professionals, and your financial success will attract these professionals. Before you start assembling the right advisors for your needs, though, it is best to clarify some of your wealth priorities. In the next chapter, we will explore your money values.

CHAPTER 2

Creating Order out of Chaos

Cluttered wealth is wealth that has lost its direction. Gaining control and getting back on track can feel overwhelming. Take the first step by considering your money values.

A LOST OPPORTUNITY

Recently a woman came to see me about setting up a personal retirement account before her taxes were due. She had done some consulting work the year before and wanted to put some of that income away for her retirement. But after researching the options online, she could not determine the correct choice for her circumstances. Though she had mentioned the additional income to her accountant in the previous year, he had not prescribed any specific action for her, perhaps because he didn't consider the matter his responsibility.

Normally she would have had several options. Based on the amount of income she projected, an individual 401(k) would have been by far the best choice. Unfortunately, now that we were entering tax season of the following year, it was too late for this option. She was forced to utilize the less efficient SEP-IRA, and this mistake was going to cost her thousands of dollars in lost retirement benefits.

These are the kinds of frustrating slip-ups that are occurring more and more frequently. Too many people have difficulty understanding their portfolios, yet too few people surround themselves with experts who will help them. They haphazardly assemble cluttered portfolios that they have difficulty managing alone. And even though many people are aware of this problem, surprisingly few take the necessary steps to solve it. What's holding them back? I find that the three most common obstacles are

- Procrastination
- Habit
- Desire for control

PROCRASTINATION

The most common obstacle that holds people back from confronting their wealth clutter is procrastination. Maybe you don't know what to do first or where to look for help, so you never get started at all. Just as you might delay cleaning out that garage because the task seems so overwhelming, you keep postponing taking control of your wealth.

To counter your procrastination, we are going to break the job down into understandable, manageable steps. You probably don't procrastinate because you don't care or because you minimize the importance of managing your wealth. You procrastinate because it is so hard to know where to start. You are starting right here and now.

HABIT

Another obstacle arises when certain approaches to investing become a habit. You have been taught from the mass media and other sources that finances should be handled a certain way. You may think you are open to considering an alternative investment approach, but then you think to yourself, "I've done pretty well so far, so why should I change?"

We do not need to change your ways. Instead we are going to help you build a strong framework to support them. Along the way you may consider some different approaches to your wealth management, but more importantly, you are going to add a few new ways of thinking about your wealth. These steps will support your approach even more, increasing your confidence through different economic and market environments.

DESIRE FOR CONTROL

Some people simply like the independence that comes from making their own investment decisions without consulting advisors. You do not consider your approach a compromise. Rather, you see it as the best way to maintain control over your most valuable assets.

A desire for control also carries an element of trust. More than likely, you have worked hard to be so successful, and you may not trust others to direct your wealth. This is understandable, and as you begin to focus on your important lifestyle and legacy goals, you may view the daily management of your wealth slightly differently. Although you may want to continue to control each decision, you may also decide that once you have a very clear vision of what is important to you, other professionals can lighten your burden without really reducing your control.

Are there other obstacles keeping you from simplifying your wealth? A goals-oriented approach to managing your wealth will help you identify your priorities and use them to overcome your obstacles along the way to steady decision making.

IDENTIFYING YOUR MONEY VALUES

Even before you begin to consider your priorities and investment goals, you should take some time to contemplate what money means to you. This may seem a simple question, but in fact, we rarely think about how we view money, the role money plays in our lives, and how our major life decisions are affected by these views.

Though we often don't think about it (and we almost never talk about it), money means different things to everyone. Our feelings about money are shaped by our parents, our grandparents, our personal experiences, and the media. Our gut attitudes about spending and saving reflect our money values. People with different money values will consider big purchases differently, identify goals differently, and think about financial risks differently.

COUPLES CAN TRIP ACROSS DIFFERENT MONEY VALUES

I work with a couple who came to me when they were starting out and enjoying the early days of a successful marriage. I suggested we talk a little about the different ways they viewed money, as I find this very helpful when working with young couples. I opened the conversation by asking the wife to describe her husband's spending habits.

She told me about their recent purchase of a new car. They had agreed that they needed a new car, and he volunteered to get it. She was very happy that he offered to make this purchase without her as she did not enjoy the car-buying process. He arrived home very happy with his purchase. The car was a compact sedan as they had discussed, but at this point in the story her tone changed. The car was loaded with premium features and technology, and she couldn't believe that he had been talked into buying all these upgrades.

The husband shook his head as he had already heard this complaint a number of times. So I asked him about the purchase. He said he was surprised by her reaction to the car because he believed he had purchased the car they had agreed upon. At this point I asked him to tell me about the cars his family had owned when he was growing up. He described mid- and full-sized cars that his family bought or leased new every few years. They had very similar features to what he had purchased. Based on his experiences, he had cautiously bought a smaller car than he was used to.

When I asked the wife about the cars her family had owned, she described them as comfortable but not feature-rich. Her family bought and drove them for years until they broke down. Clearly, this young couple brought very different money values to the car purchase.

Couples with different money values can get along splendidly for long stretches of time, until large and important financial questions arise. If a couple has never identified and shared their money values, they can easily get frustrated at each other's financial habits, viewing them as stingy or extravagant, or perhaps irresponsible or overly cautious. If you want to clear out the clutter in your wealth portfolio, you must first explore the values that will help you determine what excesses to throw out and what important priorities to keep.

This is just as you might find when you face that overcrowded garage; you may reach first to discard the unused lawn mower only to find your spouse passionately labeling it a necessity. "You never know when we might stop employing the landscaper," your spouse may reply. Before you can make wise decisions, you must first understand the money values that each of you brings to your wealth.

MONEY VALUES

What does money mean to you? What excites you about your money? What uses of your money are most satisfying for you? What financial worries do you have? Does your wealth cause you to be involved or isolated? In fact, most people's answers to these questions lead them to one of four broad money values. Perhaps you will see yourself in one of these values.

SECURITY

At some point in your life, you learned about financial struggles. Either you experienced them personally or you heard stories from your family history. You understand the challenge of having to count pennies to pay for lunch each week, meet the utility bill, or make the loan payment. Whatever the experience might have been, you fear not having enough money. For you, extra wealth in the bank is security for an unexpected emergency. No matter how much wealth you accumulate, you always fear that it will not be enough to support you and your family for the rest of your life. When thinking about money, you are likely to ask yourself, "What if something happens?"

If your primary money value is security, you probably think mostly about risks to your wealth. You will want to insure many of the financial risks in your life. When it comes to your investment portfolio, you will want to consider carefully your comfort with market risks and any specific risks in your life. When discussing investments with a financial advisor, you may have a tendency to prefer choices that preserve capital or produce steady income. This may be appropriate if your wealth is extensive enough to meet all your goals. Otherwise, you may need to embrace enough risk to allow your wealth to grow and support your lifestyle goals for many years to come.

SELF-SUFFICIENCY AND INDEPENDENCE

From your first lemonade stand to your first after-school job, earning your own money made you feel independent. When you rented your first apartment, you couldn't imagine ever living at home or in a dorm again. You love the feeling of taking care of yourself and making money decisions that no one else can question. For you, money means independence and self-sufficiency. As your wealth has grown, you are likely to ask yourself, "When will I have earned enough to be able to walk away from this job any day I choose?"

If your primary money value is independence, you probably evaluate your wealth regularly and perhaps use planning software or your own calculations to determine where your wealth might be in five or ten years. You do not fear losing your wealth, nor do you cherish it as a prize. Rather, you view it as a means to an enjoyable life. When you consider your investment portfolio, you will likely be comfortable taking the necessary risk to reach your long-term goals. Since you expect to add to your wealth each year, you will benefit from embracing a disciplined strategy and committing to that strategy regardless of short-term market movements. Your biggest risk is that you may be tempted to redefine your wealth goals every time you close in on the current goal. As your wealth grows, you will also be ready to consider estate planning and philanthropic strategies that serve your legacy goals.

SUCCESS

When you led your team to win the regional championship, everyone was impressed. You loved that feeling of pride that accompanies success. Now as an adult, financial success defines your personal success. As you have accumulated more wealth, you see it as a reflection of your success in life. When thinking about money, you usually say to yourself, "When I accumulate X, that will be real success."

If your primary money value is success, you need to always appreciate your successes. A sustainable wealth program requires a long-term commitment to your goals. You will have no problem imagining your goals, but you need to appreciate achieving them too. As you plan your investment portfolio, you may have a tendency to judge short-term performance ahead of the long-term strategy. You will need to find a financial advisor that can help you stay disciplined in your approach while also helping you see your successes along the way. Those who view money as a measure of success can sometimes lose track of other ways their life has value. Of course, you are not the value of your investment portfolio, but very successful people sometimes lose sight of other ways to value their success. As your wealth reaches the levels where it can fully support your goals, you may want to enjoy a deeper commitment to strategic philanthropy where you can experience the success your wealth and personal efforts bring to others.

OPPORTUNITY

Perhaps with your first full-time job, you were able to take your first trip abroad or pay for your first ticket to a concert at Carnegie Hall. Whatever you did with your accumulated savings, it gave you a new experience. For you, wealth presents unlimited opportunities. Your goal may be to broaden your life with travel, unique experiences, or even the newest gadget. Wealth allows you and your family to live beyond the basics and consider many possibilities. When you think about money, you may say to yourself, "If I lose it all, I will lose opportunities, but I won't lose my day-to-day life."

If your primary money value is opportunity, you will be open to the many different paths your wealth can open for you. You may have an easy time identifying goals, but you will need to work to prioritize a few in order to build a sustainable investment strategy. You are likely to be comfortable with a bit more risk in your investment portfolio as you view your growing wealth as your future potential. You can probably embrace an approach that might move up and down with short-term market cycles. As your wealth grows, you may tend to wait longer than others to start estate and philanthropic planning. This is not because you procrastinate, but because you will likely take advantage of your free time and good health to enjoy the many different opportunities your wealth affords you.

SHARING MONEY VALUES

Did you discover yourself in these most common money values? If you have difficulty discussing financial matters with your advisors honestly and openly, perhaps these descriptions helped you identify some characteristics and words to make the discussions easier. At your next meeting, you might introduce the idea that you have been considering your money values. You can share that you have determined your primary values, and you would like to review how your wealth plan reflects your values.

MONEY VALUES FOR COUPLES

If you have a spouse or partner, I encourage you both to review this section individually and then share with each other what you learned. You may discover the reasons behind your spending and saving differences. As in the story involving the young couple, it is very common for couples to have very different views of money that they might rarely discuss. Often years can slip by before a husband and wife discover they value money differently, especially when the family is materially successful.

I have found it very difficult for couples to agree on shared long-term financial goals when they do not understand each other's money values. You may be focusing on security in your old age, while your partner is thinking about opportunities to travel and experience new cultures. I have participated in discussions in which a couple initially seems to share such different financial goals. When I hear these discussions, I know that we need to step back and identify money values. Now is the time for you to understand what deep-rooted values drive both your financial decisions. When you understand more fully how you both value your wealth, you can begin to build shared goals.

SETTING YOUR GOALS

Once you determine what money represents to you, you're ready to develop goals that align with those values. By embracing a goals-oriented approach you can evaluate your financial progress on a continuing basis compared to what's most important to you, achieving your personal financial goals. Instead of worrying about whether your funds are with the right brokers, you can build a strategy that ensures all of your assets—your liquid investments, your insurance policies, your estate plans, and other components of your wealth—are pulling in the same direction.

CHAPTER 3

Dreaming of Your Leisure, Lifestyle, and Legacy

Outperforming the market is not a useful investment goal. Instead, wealth goals need to be personally meaningful and measurable. Start by thinking about your goals in terms of the "Three L's": your Leisure years, your Lifestyle years, and your Legacy years.

CAN YOU BEAT THE MARKET?

After my investment workshop, an attendee approached me and said, "I'm unhappy with my current advisor. Would you take a look at my portfolio and see if you can help?" This gentleman had attained considerable wealth, which he was managing with the help of quite a number of different advisors. He pulled out his list of investments and pointed to one. "I may want you to manage this one. It hasn't been beating the market for the last couple of years."

I pointedly but politely said to him, as I have said to many potential clients, "Who cares whether you're beating the market? The real question is whether you are achieving your goals."

This comment launched a long conversation. I asked him how his entire portfolio was doing and what he was trying to achieve. Despite his level of wealth, he had no overall plan. He evaluated each of his money managers individually against the criteria of whether they were beating the market.

I explained to him that outperforming the market should never be the primary measure of success. "If you decided you wanted to lose weight," I asked him, "would you say, 'I want to lose enough weight to conform to the medical tables for a person of my height and age?' Probably not! Neither would you say, 'I want to be skinnier than my neighbor.' More likely you'd say, 'I want to lose so many pounds.'"

Almost any goal we set for ourselves in life is personal. We rarely determine goals on a relative basis. Yet, we've been trained to assess our investments relative to arbitrarily established benchmarks that have nothing to do with our personal goals.

Take the S&P 500 Index, for example. The Standard & Poor's Corporation established this index of 500 stocks in 1957. Although the stocks included in the index are chosen according to certain criteria, a fair amount of subjectivity is involved in the committee-based selection process in which member stocks are updated and changed quarterly. Does it really make sense to measure the performance of your investment portfolio by comparing it to such a benchmark?

Additionally, a benchmark never incurs trading costs when it adds or removes securities. A benchmark never adds or withdraws funds, and a benchmark is not subject to capital gains and dividend taxes. How can you measure your personal progress against such artificial conditions?

When cleaning out your cluttered clothes closet, you certainly want to consider whether those pants are still in fashion. But more importantly, you need to know whether they still fit you, reflect the look you want, and will get wear in your current lifestyle. Like your clothes, your financial goals need to fit you and reflect your personal priorities. Now that you have considered your money values, in this chapter we will introduce a framework for formulating your financial goals. These goals are the foundation for managing your wealth with purpose, clarity, and consistency.

YOUR THREE L GOALS

I have worked with many clients who come to me after years of being trained by the mass-media approach to investments. When I suggest that we discuss their goals, they often quickly reply, "I want growth with moderate risk." This is not a wealth goal.

I turn the conversation by suggesting that we discuss their vision of the future. You, too, may find it easier to think about and prioritize your financial goals in the context of the future life you envision. To facilitate this process, I suggest considering the future in terms of the following three major stages of our adult lives:

- Your Leisure Years
- Your Lifestyle Years
- Your Legacy Years

LEISURE GOALS

Leisure goals are those goals that are above and beyond your everyday working lifestyle. These are goals that enhance your life experiences while you are still committing much of your time to a career and, perhaps, to raising a family. Since your income supports your everyday lifestyle, your leisure goals shift your focus from needs to preferences. If you're like most people, your leisure goals will be those you wish to attain between now and your late sixties to early seventies.

Leisure goals tend to encompass both aspirational purchases and experiential goals. Typical purchase goals might include additional homes, automobiles, boats, planes, and investment properties. They might also include building satisfying collections such as art, classic automobiles, precious ceramics, or antiques. Experiential leisure goals might include things such as traveling, joining a hands-on effort in developing countries, or supporting your children's ventures.

Of the three L's, your leisure goals will have the shortest time horizon. Some goals you might want to achieve within a year or two, and others will take somewhat longer. Just keep in mind that these are goals that are above and beyond your current lifestyle.

Since leisure goals enhance your existing life, they are most sensitive to your money values. If you or your spouse value money mostly as security, you are less likely to consider and embrace lots of leisure goals. Instead, you will prefer to preserve your wealth for your future lifestyle and legacy goals. If you value money as a means of independence or opportunity, you might put more priority on leisure goals that enhance your current life experiences.

LIFESTYLE GOALS

Lifestyle goals pertain to the time of life—usually from sometime in your late fifties or sixties well into your eighties—when you'll be living almost entirely off the wealth you have accumulated. When planning for lifestyle goals, you want to first consider the lifestyle you envision later in life. Your primary concern is to ensure that you accumulate adequate resources to support the lifestyle you desire.

Since your lifestyle goals are likely to be a number of years off, it's wise to start planning for them now. Do you envision staying in your current home, or have you pondered moving to a new geographic area? Do you hope to build your dream house, or do you plan to downsize and outsource household maintenance? Perhaps you hope to sail your lifestyle years up and down the coast.

Lifestyle goals can make everyone a bit anxious. Many people worry that they may not have enough money to live out their life, no matter how much wealth they have. This concern is common and understandable. As you think about your lifestyle goals, start by realistically imagining a lifestyle that is not dramatically different from your current one. The geography, housing, and activities may be different, but unless you anticipate an event that will significantly change your wealth, keep your expectations realistic.

LEGACY GOALS

Because legacy goals have the longest time frames, they're usually the hardest goals to think about. It's wise to start your planning process for them as early as practical, so that you and other members of your family will have time to harmonize your visions. For example, if your spouse wants to leave your wealth primarily to philanthropic organizations, whereas you want to pass it on to your children, it's wise to address these differences sooner rather than later.

Similarly, as you establish your legacy goals, you will want to clearly identify your priorities and communicate your values. What are you trying to achieve with your gifts? How would you like to see your wealth spent? You may want to consider your legacy in three major areas:

- Keeping Wealth within the Family
- Giving Wealth to Support the Greater Good
- Using Your Wealth to Create a Lasting Legacy

Keeping Wealth within the Family

When you think about passing on wealth to your children and grandchildren, inevitably your values will come into play. Most people want to do more than simply distribute money to their loved ones; they want to thoughtfully wrap every gift to their children and grandchildren in their values. This may mean providing guidance about how your gifts will be used. If you hope your gifts will encourage future behavior, then consider what activities you want to support. What entrepreneurial ventures, artistic endeavors, educational opportunities, or other activities do you believe would be good for them to pursue? Are there charities or community services you would encourage them to support?

It is very common to have concerns about gifts to some of your children or grandchildren. Some children need money more than others. Some children are ready to handle money, while other children repeatedly make poor financial decisions. There is no need to feel reluctant to express these concerns. You may decide to share your concerns with your children and let them know early on that you want to work with them to improve their financial management skills. You can also start thinking about how you might want to adjust your gifting plans over time if you feel your heir can't adequately manage an inheritance. Eventually, you may decide it is necessary to structure your legacy gift in a way that assures benefits to your child(ren), but includes the guidance of an experienced financial steward or trustee.

Giving Wealth to Support the Greater Good

Warren Buffet and Bill Gates have challenged the wealthiest families in the world to give at least half of their wealth to charity. Perhaps you want to embrace this commitment as well. Like all of your legacy goals, this is something you should begin considering now. It may take a number of years to fully define your charitable goals.

Many of the most established charitable organizations have experienced philanthropic planners that can help you think about the kind of gift that feels meaningful. They can also help you consider the various ways to make such a charitable commitment while your wealth is still accumulating.

Using Your Wealth to Create a Lasting Legacy

Perhaps you want your wealth to create a lasting legacy, but what kind of legacy? You may want to create a financial legacy for your family by means of a trust that maintains your wealth for many generations. Perhaps you have philanthropic goals in which you would like to create an enduring legacy. Do you want to set up a family foundation that future generations will manage to support causes you believe in? If so what charities, educational institutions, or societal causes do you want to support? Perhaps you want your legacy to be recognized in the community by pledging your wealth to a future project that will bear your family name.

Any of these strategies may create lasting legacies that celebrate your financial success for years to come. Committing your wealth to these kinds of legacy goals may take many years of consideration. It is good to start talking about your thoughts and sharing these priorities with the rest of your family to gain feedback and acceptance of your wishes.

REFINING YOUR GOALS

After you've compiled a list of as many goals as you can imagine, you will want to refine it by reducing the number of goals and increasing the descriptive details. As you work through your list of goals, you will want to eventually assign a time frame and a value to each. Therefore, you will want to hone your goals to be as specific as possible.

As you consider each goal, you will probably notice that a number of items begin to naturally group themselves. For example, a few dreams might be thought of as slices of a greater goal. After a bit of reorganization and consolidation, you'll probably end up with a list of three to five major statements that encapsulate your wealth goals.

For purposes of illustration, here are the financial priority goals for my clients, Jim and Lisa, rising executives who are still working and raising their children:

- Send two children to the colleges of their choice.
- Support future lifestyle completely starting at age 60.
- Provide health care and lifestyle support to parents for the next 10 to 15 years.

Another illustration comes from Mike and Susan, a successful couple in their early seventies:

- Support current lifestyle without reducing investment capital.
- Fund college for six grandchildren.
- Preserve and build wealth for future generations to enjoy.

ASSIGNING TIME FRAMES

The next step in refining your goals is to start assigning time frames to your goals. When do you need to achieve each one? For some goals, that may be quite soon. Perhaps college is only two years off for one of your children. Maybe you'll be looking at a change in career or lifestyle in five years. Each goal should have a specific time frame, or, if you prefer, more simply classified by your Three L's.

Here are our couples' goals updated with time frames:

Jim and Lisa in Their Leisure Years

	GOAL	TIME FRAME
1	Send two children to the colleges of their choice.	2–8 years
2	Support future lifestyle completely starting at age 60.	Lifestyle years (15 years)
3	Provide health care and lifestyle support to parents for next 10 to 15 years.	5–15 years

Mike and Susan in Their Lifestyle Years

	GOAL	TIME FRAME
1	Support current lifestyle without reducing capital.	0–25 years
2	Fund college for six grandchildren.	8–24 years
3	Preserve and build wealth for future generations to enjoy.	Legacy years (20+ years)

By assigning time frames, you can more readily see that these families have some near- term wealth needs. Other goals will not be fulfilled for many years, which will allow time for their wealth to continue to accumulate. Once you reach this point, you will begin to have an increasingly clear view of how to think about your wealth now and in the future.

ALLOCATING YOUR WEALTH

You are now ready to share your financial goals with a professional financial advisor. The advisor will lead you through the final steps of confirming that your goals are achievable, discussing what it will take to achieve these goals and allocating your current and future wealth to them.

If you are comfortable with numbers and would like to work independently, there are steps you can take to gain a greater understanding of what it will take to achieve your goals. While no calculation is an exact science, you can make some reasonable estimates using the following information:

- Current wealth
- Years to goal
- Current cost

- Estimated annual investment return

You will need a spreadsheet computer program, a calculator with financial functions, or an online savings calculator. You can find a simple and useful savings calculator at money.msn.com.

SHORT-TERM GOALS

For shorter-term goals, such as a new car, a new house, or funding for college, start with an estimate of what it would cost to achieve that goal today. Then estimate how much inflation and other factors will influence these costs in the intervening years. Historically, for example, the cost of a college education has increased each year at two to three times the rate of inflation.

Jim and Lisa might start by assuming that four years of private college today costs $50,000 per year. Their first child will be off to school in two years, and their second will start in five years. With a calculator, they can determine how the total cost will increase if inflation is estimated at 3%. At twice the rate of inflation, or 6% per year, what costs $50,000 per year in today's dollars could cost much more tomorrow, as shown in the following table.

College Tuition

	CHILD ONE (2 YEARS OUT)	CHILD TWO (5 YEARS OUT)
Year 1	$56,180	$70,925
Year 2	$59,551	$75,181
Year 3	$63,124	$79,692
Year 4	$66,911	$84,473

What might cost a total of $400,000 in total today is likely to cost this family over $550,000 by the time their second child completes four years of college. If the family and their advisor determine that they can reasonably expect to grow their investments 6%, they can allocate $400,000 to this goal. If they follow an investment strategy that contemplates a higher or lower annual rate of return, they will allocate a different amount of wealth to this goal.

LIFESTYLE GOALS

Calculating the amount of wealth you'll need for your lifestyle goals is often tricky for several reasons. First, these goals are typically quite long-range, which can make it difficult to predict the effects of inflation and other variables. Second, calculations of lifestyle wealth leave little margin for error. Any mistake in your calculations now can cause significant problems later.

First, you should consider how your desired future lifestyle compares to the lifestyle you enjoy today. Can you estimate whether that lifestyle will cost less than your current lifestyle? Many retirement calculators suggest that your retirement life will cost 70 to 80% of your working lifestyle. However, you have had a very successful life so far, and it is likely that your lifestyle may even cost a bit more once you have some extra time to enjoy it. As long as you stay healthy, you may find that your lifestyle costs will remain high until you approach your legacy years.

Start with an estimate of the cost of your current lifestyle. Mike and Susan are just starting to fund their lifestyle. Let's estimate their annual lifestyle cost at $250,000. They are likely to enjoy life for at least 25 more years. If we assume an annual rate of inflation of 3%, their lifestyle will cost them over $9 million over those 25 years. Their question, however, is how much do they need today to fund that. Well, that depends on their reasonable investment plans. Here is an example of the different amounts needed today depending on the annual return expectations:

Investing for Lifetime Goals

ESTIMATED ANNUAL RETURN %	WEALTH NEEDED TO SUPPORT LIFESTYLE
4.0%	$3,905,520
5.0%	$3,523,486
6.0%	$3,195,839
7.0%	$2,913,396
8.0%	$2,668,694

As you can see, the numbers can vary dramatically between $2.7M to $3.9M. That is quite a difference today! When you try this exercise, if your plans require annual returns of 7% or more, you might want to rethink your lifestyle expectations. While it is true that the long-term returns in the stock market have averaged 9 to 10%, that has certainly not been achieved consistently. If your first few lifestyle years hit a rocky stock market, your plans could quickly go awry. And it is likely that your investment strategy will use a mix of investments, not just stocks.

YOUR GOALS DEFINE YOUR WEALTH PLAN

When you have identified your three to five major goals, it is useful to make a chart that shows each goal, the time frame, and the wealth needed. Here are the charts for our two families:

Jim and Lisa's Goals

	GOAL	TIME FRAME	WEALTH
1	Send two children to the colleges of their choice.	2–8 years	$0.5M
2	Support future lifestyle completely starting at age 60.	Lifestyle years (15 years)	$1.6M
3	Provide health care and lifestyle support for parents for the next 10 to 15 years.	5–10 years	$1.1M

Mike and Susan's Goals

	GOAL	TIME FRAME	WEALTH
1	Support current lifestyle without reducing capital.	0–25 years	$3.2M
2	Fund college for six grandchildren.	8–24 years	$1.5M
3	Preserve and build wealth for future generations to enjoy.	Legacy years	$1.0M available

Look over your own goals table to see what it will take for you to accomplish your goals. Are they achievable? If so, you will no doubt feel encouraged. If not, you may have to make some adjustments. You may even realize that you must make immediate changes to your lifestyle in order to preserve money for the future.

It's important to be realistic. To get back to our losing weight analogy, some people might think it would be nice to lose thirty pounds, when losing ten pounds might be healthier and more likely. You should be equally thoughtful as you carry out this exercise with your portfolio.

Most of my clients start feeling much more empowered after this goal-setting exercise. It is an important step in letting go of the clutter. Instead of spending your time trying to understand how to read a broker's report or prospectus, you can begin to focus on what you want to do with your wealth. And as you switch your concentration to the steps to achieve your goals, you will feel more in control. After all, wealth management is about more than simply managing your investment portfolio. It's about utilizing your wealth to achieve the life and legacy that bring you satisfaction.

CHAPTER 4

Building Your Wealth Inventory

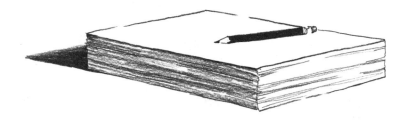

Your wealth consists of more than investments. A wealth inventory will help you identify all your assets and liabilities and organize your affairs. Armed with a complete inventory, your net worth statement will help you see the big picture.

You've taken the first steps to clearing the clutter in your wealth by clarifying your financial goals. Like cleaning out your garage, you've made decisions about what major items to keep or to toss. Now what's left behind may or may not survive, and the only way to be sure is to start to organize it. With wealth planning, the organizing step is creating your wealth inventory.

Your wealth consists of more than your investments; it includes everything you own and everything you owe. A wealth inventory, therefore, is a list of every one of your assets and your liabilities and their ownership. It is both a financial snapshot and a wealth-organizing document. Before you can construct a wealth plan to achieve your goals, you need a current and complete accounting of your wealth.

Do you have an up-to-date list of your insurance policies, checking and savings accounts, investment portfolios, real estate holdings, automobiles, and other assets? Do you have concise records of your liabilities, including mortgages, credit lines, and margin debt? Are the contact information for your advisors and the numbers and passwords for your accounts readily accessible to you?

Without a comprehensive picture of your wealth, it's difficult to develop a sound financial strategy. When you must hunt for information before you can make each financial decision, you may end up missing opportunities and omitting important data. And of course, you can waste a tremendous amount of time when you must pour through old files over and over again to track down the information you need. Having this information at your fingertips can save you valuable time and help you avoid costly mistakes.

ASSEMBLING THE PIECES

Here is a list of the most common items that you should include on your net worth statement. You may have even more items:

Financial Assets

- Savings, checking, and CD accounts

- Investment accounts
- Retirement accounts
- Executive compensation accounts

Insurance Products

- Life insurance (cash value)
- Annuities

Personal Property

- Homes
- Autos
- Boats/planes
- Collectibles

Debt

- Mortgages
- Lines of credit
- Auto loans
- Margin debt
- Credit card debt

Don't overlook the assets and liabilities of your spouse and any custodial accounts of your children. Include any art, antiques, or other collector's items you may own that have enough value to be part of your long-term investment portfolio.

PUTTING IT TOGETHER

Creating a wealth inventory is a little like assembling a jigsaw puzzle. First, get all the pieces together—all your files, statements, and contact information. For each of the assets and debts on your list, you will want to assemble the following information:

- Exact title on asset or account

- Account number
- Value
- Contact information of advisor

Next begin fitting the pieces into the puzzle little by little. Start with the easiest pieces— the big ones around the edges—and keep filling in until you have a completed picture. I suggest using a template, or worksheet, to help you organize all the pieces. Some people like a written format, such as the one I've included in Appendix A. Others prefer a computer program, such as Quicken™. You can also download my worksheet from our clutter-free website.

Your completed net worth statement might look like this:

Sample Wealth Inventory

ACCOUNT	SPOUSE 1	SPOUSE 2	JOINT	TOTAL
Taxable Marketable Assets				
Checking	$0	$0	$250,236	$250,236
Living Trust	$1,449,073	$0	$0	$1,449,073
Living Trust	$0	$1,345,337	$0	$1,345,337
Employee Options	$873,687	$0	$0	$873,687
Sub Total	$2,322,760	$1,345,337	$250,236	$3,918,333
Tax-Deferred Marketable Securities				
401K	$724,522	$0	$0	$724,522
Sub Total	$724,522	$0	$0	$724,522
Tax-Exempt Marketable Assets				
Roth IRA	$82,076	$0	$0	$82,076
Roth IRA	$0	$803,182	$0	$803,182
Sub Total	$82,076	$803,182	$0	$885,258
Business Assets				
LLC Ownership	$0	$775,000	$0	$775,000
Family Assets				
Ltd Partnership	$0	$0	$1,284,334	$1,284,334
FLP Real Estate	$0	$0	$869,336	$869,336
Sub Total	$0	$0	$2,153,670	$2,153,670
Real Estate Holdings				
Real Estate 1	$775,000	$0	$0	$775,000
Real Estate 2	$0	$1,272,000	$0	$1,272,000
Sub Total	$775,000	$1,272,000	$0	$2,047,000
TOTAL ASSETS	$3,904,358	$4,195,519	$2,403,906	$10,503,783
Debt				
Mortgage on RE 2	$0	$351,722	$0	$351,722
Mortgage on FLP	$0	$0	$271,668	$271,668
TOTAL DEBT	$0	$351,722	$271,668	$623,390
TOTAL NET WORTH	$3,904,358	$3,843,797	$2,132,238	$9,880,393

When you're done, you're likely to feel even more comfortable and confident as your financial affairs start becoming organized. And in the years ahead, this inventory will allow you to make better decisions that support your goals. Speaking of "the years ahead," plan to update your wealth inventory regularly. A good advisor will do this with you, but make an appointment with yourself and put it on your calendar.

You will now be ready to share your wealth inventory and wealth goals with your professional advisors. If you don't have your best team in place, in the next chapter we will discuss how to identify and select the right professionals for your needs. A well-coordinated team will help you construct and maintain a comprehensive, disciplined wealth plan.

CHAPTER 5

Assembling Your Team

A successful professional team starts with a quarter-back who will coordinate your affairs. That person is likely to be your financial advisor, but choosing one can be particularly confusing with so many titles and so many credentials. To help you find qualified professionals, use these 10 questions when you interview your prospective advisors.

My first job title was analyst. Over the years I became a portfolio manager, a vice president, and a managing director. Only my most junior titles told anyone what I did professionally. When I was managing mutual funds at Oppenheimer Funds, I was encouraged to seek my CFA designation. For the next three years I studied full time while working and earned the coveted designation of Chartered Financial Analyst. Back then, not too many people outside my profession understood what CFA meant, but others within my profession now understood completely that I specialized in analyzing and selecting investments. As my career progressed and clients started asking more and more varied financial questions of me, I decided to pursue my CFP® certification. As a Certified Financial Planner, I augmented my deep investment expertise with a broad understanding of the many facets of wealth management. I am currently known as Elizabeth K. Miller, CFA & CFP®, President of Summit Place Financial Advisors, LLC. Can you tell what I do?

Finding financial professionals can be a very confusing exercise. If you think your portfolio is cluttered, it's nothing compared to the obfuscation in the financial services industry. Now that you are clear on your goals, though, it's time to start bringing some financial professionals into your life. You should assemble a team that includes a financial advisor, a trust and estate attorney, an accountant, and an insurance professional. Each of these should be individually qualified and focused only on their area of expertise.

YOUR QUARTERBACK

As you work through this book, we are going to reduce the clutter in your wealth plan, clean out the big unused items, and sweep out the back dark corners. To keep it that way in the future, you need someone who will act as your financial quarterback. Sometimes this role is known as your trusted advisor.

A trusted advisor understands your full wealth portfolio and your goals. This professional will regularly look at your cleaned-out garage and make recommendations about the fresh contents. Do you have room to hang another bicycle in back? Would things be more organized if you hung a row of wall cabinets?

Most often, this person is your financial professional or your trust and estate attorney. Both of these professionals tend to have deep expertise in their own field, yet they have accumulated knowledge of the other disciplines. As your trusted advisor, they can help you consider strategies in all parts of your wealth. They can make recommendations and help you identify the questions that need to be answered by other appropriate professionals.

The most committed trusted advisors will usually communicate with all your allied professionals to keep them up to date on your status. Often, they will initiate conversations with a professional when you have a new idea to discuss, so that your meeting time is not prolonged by background information and introductions.

If you are unclear about whether your attorney or financial advisor is willing to step into this role, then you are probably working with someone who is not capable of being your quarterback. Trusted advisor professionals make it clear that they are ready to take on this responsibility as part of the service they provide.

As you interview your professionals, be watchful for your quarterback. Once you identify this professional, they can usually recommend your other professionals. Below are some thoughts for identifying each professional, and at the end of this chapter are ten questions you can use to interview all candidates for your professional team.

YOUR FINANCIAL ADVISOR

The financial services industry can be very confusing because professional titles are not standardized. Here is a list of common titles a financial professional might use to describe themselves. Have you employed any of these people in the past?

- **Broker**—Traditionally, a broker is someone who earns a commission for recommending investment products.

- **Financial Advisor/Financial Consultant**—These are generic titles that can apply to any professional. At several of the large brokerage firms, "financial consultant" has replaced the title "broker."
- **Financial Planner**—Planners help you identify goals and achieve them. Most planners have another financial specialty such as insurance sales, investment management, or accounting.
- **Money Manager/Portfolio Manager**—A money manager/portfolio manager usually has experience making investment decisions in an account, including selecting individual investments and executing trades.
- **Registered Investment Advisor (RIA)**—A registered investment advisor is a firm that has registered with the Security and Exchange Commission or a state authority as a business that takes fiduciary responsibility for its clients' investments. An RIA is NOT a person, but the firm that employs financial professionals.
- **Private Banker**—A private banker is typically a client service representative associated with a commercial banking institution. The person is dedicated to providing personal service and coordinates access to the services and products available at the institution.

These are the most popular titles you may hear, but this is not an exhaustive list of the descriptions financial professionals will use. Unfortunately, you cannot tell from the title which of these professionals may or may not be appropriate for you.

FINANCIAL CERTIFICATIONS

Financial professionals will further confuse you with their certifications. While all continuing education for a professional should be appreciated, there are really just a few certifications that you should value as you look for a financial professional. Here they are:

- **Chartered Financial Analyst (CFA)**—This is the designation of investment professionals offered by CFA Institute. CFA charterholders have earned a university degree, have met professional work requirements, and have successfully passed three annual, 6-hour exams that test all areas of investment analysis, selection, and portfolio construction. The examinations also include a strong ethics component, and charterholders must annually sign a Standards of Professional Conduct Statement.

- **Certified Financial Planner (CFP®)**—This designation, offered by the Certified Financial Planner Board of Standards, Inc., emphasizes individual planning with a broad knowledge of all areas of personal finance. A CFP® must earn a bachelor's degree, meet learning requirements, and pass a 10-hour exam. To use the designation, a CFP® must meet both work and ethics requirements and pursue continuing education.

- **Certified Investment Management Analyst (CIMA)**—This certification is most often sought by Series 7 licensed securities sales professionals (traditionally known as brokers) and is offered by the Investment Management Consultants Association (IMCA). The CIMA certification provides a broad knowledge of portfolio construction and performance analysis. A CIMA must have three years of relevant experience and must first pass a qualification examination. Next is a five-day classroom educational requirement followed by an online certification exam. The certificatant also signs a Code of Professional Responsibility.

Now that you have de-cluttered the titles and ABCs of many financial professionals, it is time to start homing in on the right professional for you. The first important decision you need to make is whether you want to operate on a discretionary or nondiscretionary basis. Let's discuss each of these two options in turn.

A NONDISCRETIONARY ADVISOR

Often called a broker, a nondiscretionary advisor does not have the independent authority (discretion) to make changes to your portfolio. These professionals are referred to as registered representatives because they are registered with a governing body as sales representatives for their organization.

A nondiscretionary advisor will recommend investments to you based on your goals and your expressed tolerance for risk. If you say yes, the advisor will then help you purchase these securities. Many advisors will provide some amount of ongoing management advice if you so desire, but it is considered incidental to their overall business. Legally, this professional is held to a "suitability" requirement. This means that the advisor is obligated to ensure that the investments he or she recommends are suitable for you and that you are treated in a just and equitable manner compared to other clients.

Some brokers work for large institutions, which historically have been called brokerage firms. Today, many of these institutions call themselves wealth management firms, and the brokers they employ may refer to themselves as wealth advisors, financial advisors, or financial consultants.

Advisors with large firms may have access to valuable resources that can help you clarify your goals and choose the appropriate investments to attain them. However, some of their planning software and investment programs generate "cookie-cutter" recommendations that may not be adequate for wealthy investors who merit more individualized attention.

Be sure to ask how your advisor will be compensated for his or her advice and recommendations. Most brokers will be compensated based on the investment products you purchase and the transactions you authorize. You usually don't see these fees, however, because they're buried within the costs of the investment products you purchase.

A DISCRETIONARY INVESTMENT ADVISOR

The discretionary investment advisor has your authority to manage your portfolio on a day-to-day basis consistent with guidelines you have established. This type of professional, who typically works for a registered investment advisor (RIA), is first and foremost a portfolio manager, not a salesperson. Legally, this professional is held to a fiduciary standard. This means your professional is legally bound to act solely in your best interests, as a fiduciary.

After working with you to understand your financial goals, a discretionary investment advisor will help you attain them by developing an appropriate strategy and selecting the right investments. You as the investor maintain overall control because you have determined the goals and agreed upon the strategy, but you do not need to be bothered with the day-to-day operational details. Your discretionary advisor will make purchases and sales of securities when appropriate and will continually monitor your portfolio for you.

All RIAs are registered with either the SEC or a state commission. These firms may be large with a wide range of in-house or best-of-breed investments available, or they may be small boutiques that specialize in exceptional service.

Now you are ready to meet with some financial professionals who might suit your needs. You need not bring your portfolio to the initial meeting, but you should be comfortable sharing some specifics about your situation during the interview. Do not meet with any financial professional who charges you for an initial consultation!

ESTATE PLANNING ATTORNEY

Good estate planning is more than just simply drafting a will. Your estate planning needs are more complex than those of most individuals, and you will need an expert who understands the latest tax laws and informs you when changes and opportunities arise. A good estate planning professional can help you consider what kind of legacy you would like to create and how to most efficiently distribute your wealth after your death. Your attorney will help you set up contingency plans, assure that your wishes regarding health care treatment are followed, and steward your estate through probate.

Some planning firms offer to do estate planning and suggest that you will only need a licensed attorney to "draft documents." However, I strongly disagree. Your wealth demands a qualified professional with a law degree and an expertise in trusts and estates. Only this professional is a member of the bar association and has a fiduciary duty to you.

To help you locate a qualified professional, some states have a board certification program that allows attorneys to designate a specialty area such as wills, trusts, and estates. If your state does not have this specialization, you can look at an attorney's membership in bar associations and estate planning organizations as well as published writings and speaking engagements to verify their commitment to this area of expertise.

Most lawyers charge by the hour for their time. Some estate planning attorneys, however, offer a flat fee for initial estate planning documents. Both approaches are common, and you should understand the pros and cons of each. If your attorney charges by the hour, he or she will seemingly have an incentive to increase the time spent in office consultations and phone conversations. Consequently, you may find yourself limiting interaction to manage the hourly fee, which will not achieve your best plan. With an hourly billing arrangement, ask the prospective lawyer for an estimate of the time it will take to complete the documents. Inquire about what actions you might take that will expedite the process or slow it down. Also, discuss what parts of the work will be done by support staff that may have a lower hourly rate.

When there is a flat-fee arrangement, many clients fear that the attorney will deliver a less customized product or less personalized service. Usually, flat-fee arrangements are offered as a convenience and as an attempt to limit the incentives of hourly billing. In these situations, be sure to discuss what the flat fee will include. Also, just as in the hourly arrangement, ask what role your lead attorney will play and how much of the work will be done by support staff.

Whether you prefer an attorney associated with a large professional group or a small specialized practice depends on your specific needs. If you have extensive real estate holdings, you should seek out a lawyer who understands property law or has colleagues with this expertise. If you are considering a sizeable charitable legacy, look for a professional with this specialty. Always think about your unique circumstances and be prepared to ask about them in an initial interview.

ACCOUNTANT

There are two kinds of accountants: certified public accountants (CPAs) and public accountants. CPAs have passed a national exam administered in their state and have completed qualifying work experience. Your accountant will prepare your tax returns and provide ongoing tax-related advice.

Accounting firms may charge a flat fee for your tax return, or they may charge by the hour. Be sure to discuss potential fees with a prospective accountant. Even though your substantial wealth has a number of complexities, if your tax return consists primarily of simple earned income and gains and dividends from an investment portfolio, you may be well served by a small accounting group that can offer competitive fees.

The additional expertise you seek in an accountant will depend on your personal circumstances. If you own income-producing real estate, you might prefer a larger practice that has in-house expertise in real estate laws and valuations. If you are a business owner, you might prefer an accountant who can manage both your personal and business tax affairs, or you might choose a large accounting firm with different areas of expertise including business consulting. Some accounting firms these days have in-house investment planning; in my experience, it is best to keep your financial professionals and accounting professionals separate.

INSURANCE AGENT

Insurance agents are licensed by states to sell their respective products. Because agents earn a commission when they sell a policy, there have been many high-profile conflict-of-interest cases in which agents have recommended excessive changing and exchanging of insurance products. The best way to avoid this risk is to get a trusted referral from your other professionals. An experienced and knowledgeable insurance agent is very valuable.

Many insurance agents are affiliated with a single insurance provider and know that product line extremely well. Additionally, this agent may be able to meet both your health and life insurance needs as well as your property and casualty needs.

Independent agents sell products for multiple insurance companies and may be better positioned to find the best competitive product for your needs. Often, an independent agent may specialize in life and health insurance products or property and casualty products, but not both. Larger independent firms may have several professionals who can meet all your needs.

Be aware that some financial planners with the CFP® designation also become licensed to sell insurance products. You might choose this professional for your insurance needs, but I recommend using a different financial advisor for your investment needs.

REFERRALS

People often ask me how to find a trusted referral for these professionals. If you already have one of these professionals in place, that's often a good starting point for finding the others. If you are an executive in a company, your peers and other successful executives in your firm who may have already achieved the level of success to which you aspire may also be good sources of referrals. Finally, you might reach out to friends whom you believe are in similar financial circumstances.

Over time you may change professionals as your needs change. Often a successful family comes to me with one of these professionals in place. As we work together and begin to de-clutter their wealth and focus on their goals, we often discover that their needs may have outgrown the long-time professional with whom they started. This is never a judgment on that professional; it is simply an acknowledgment that changes in personal circumstances often require specific expertise to de-clutter complex wealth situations.

TEN QUESTIONS TO ASK YOUR PROSPECTIVE ADVISORS

Before you decide to work with a particular advisor, be sure to conduct your due diligence. Here are a few questions you will want to ask candidates:

1. What are your credentials (schools, advanced certifications, employment history)?
2. What licenses do you hold? Are you registered with the SEC, a state or national agency, the bar association, etc.?
3. What products and services do you offer?
4. How are you paid for your services? What is your usual hourly rate, flat fee, or commission?
5. Has any regulatory body ever disciplined you for unethical or improper conduct, or have you been sued by a client for unsatisfactory performance?
6. Will you send me a copy of both parts of your Form ADV (for registered investment advisors) or your professional disclosure?
7. What experience do you have with clients who have circumstances similar to mine?
8. How would you factor in my specific circumstances? (Discuss your business, real estate or deferred income holdings for example. Con-

sider it a yellow flag if the advisor doesn't think that these specific holdings have much bearing on your overall wealth plan.)

9. What conflicts of interest exist in your business, and how do you address them?

10. How often will you be communicating with me? How will your staff communicate with me?

CHAPTER 6

Planning for Risks

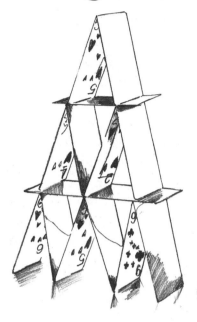

A number of risks can threaten your wealth goals including personal risks, property risks, and financial risks. Some of these can be managed with proper insurance. However, all investments have risks, so it is important to understand them and find your comfort point.

Julie and Sam came to me after purchasing two large life insurance policies with their children as beneficiaries. After consulting with an insurance professional, they realized that they needed to add a professional who could help them evaluate and achieve their overall goals. Even though they had meaningful wealth, they were worried that they might spend much of it to maintain their lifestyle and that they would have too little left to meet their legacy goals which included leaving a specified amount of money to each of their children.

Julie and Sam were identifying risks in their wealth goals. Most people have some concern that their wealth might not support them throughout their lifetime. They think about this risk usually in terms of overspending. However, there are a number of additional risks to every well-considered wealth plan. This is why you need a comprehensive risk management plan that addresses a wide range of risks. Julie and Sam had insured against only one sliver of risk without considering the other risks to their goals.

Of course, it is difficult to think about a personal risk management strategy when in reality we are talking about different insurance polices filed away in different folders and locations. Perhaps each one has a different professional provider as well. It doesn't feel like a strategy; it's a pile of paperwork.

The clutter-free approach to risk management starts with thinking about your risks through three easy categories:

1. Personal Risks
2. Property Risks
3. Investment Risks

Your risk management decisions in each of these areas reflect both your financial values and your comfort with different kinds of risk. Wealth risks should not keep you awake at night. The guiding principle should be that each of your decisions increases your comfort as well as the probability of reaching your goals. As you consider each of these areas, you will build your own cohesive risk management strategy.

PERSONAL RISKS

The first category of risk is personal risk. For example, your wealth goals may go wildly astray if you and your spouse are not taking care of your health. These are risks that are almost entirely insurable. Of course, as you review the personal insurance on your risk management plan, you might also address the lifestyle decisions that are entirely in your control, such as eating right and staying active.

START WITH YOUR HEALTH INSURANCE

Do you have a plan that adequately protects you against the costs of illness and injury? If you do not have insurance through an employer or a group, private medical insurance can be expensive, but it's also vital. It is always a good idea to regularly review this coverage for the mix of services and deductibles that best fit your priorities. These days, many successful individuals are opting for plans that have a high annual deductible and strong, unlimited coverage for catastrophic events. These plans are attractive if you can easily afford the everyday doctor visits that are needed each year while relying on the premium coverage should something unexpected occur. Other choices might emphasize stronger prescription coverage if you or a family member needs long-term medication. With pending changes in the health care laws, insurance plans are changing constantly. Don't simply accept the latest replacement for your previous plan year after year. Be sure to regularly review the range of options available.

YOU MIGHT CONSIDER LONG-TERM CARE INSURANCE

You also might want to consider acquiring long-term care insurance to cover the costs of medical assistance later in life. Studies indicate that at least one member of every couple will need long-term medical assistance. Many successful people have the means to pay these expenses out of their accumulated wealth. However, a multiyear stay in a luxury long-term care facility due to Alzheimer's or some other debilitating condition can derail some of your lifestyle or legacy goals. If you feel that you are vulnerable to this risk, reach out to a professional who can tell you about options in long-term care insurance. This is relatively inexpensive insurance and can be particularly attractive if you commit to it in your forties and fifties.

While some major insurance firms have left the long-term care business, there have also been interesting innovations in this market. A recent structure that might be attractive offers a refund of principal if the policy is not used. Another structure combines a long-term care policy with a life insurance policy that pays your family at death if the long-term care services were not required.

These policies have many different features that can add to or reduce the cost of the policy. A qualified professional will help you choose those that fit you best. One common feature of these policies is an inflation component that adds dramatically to the cost. You may not need this option as the growth in your investment portfolio can serve to offset inflation costs.

DON'T OVERLOOK DISABILITY INSURANCE

If you are still in your working years, disability insurance can provide you with a portion of your regular income in the event of a debilitating sickness or injury. Disability insurance is a must for successful executives and business owners who have built their wealth from income. If something unexpected happens, you can be left with little income for your future. A disability insurance policy gives you the confidence that you and your family will continue to enjoy the benefits of the career position you have worked so hard to attain.

Some employers offer the opportunity to purchase disability insurance. If yours does not, or if you are self-employed, it is worthwhile for you to pursue your own policy. A quality disability policy covers you until you are 65 years old and can replace a good percentage of your lost income. You will want to be sure that the policy covers you for your particular occupation, even if you may be able to seek some lesser kind of employment. The other feature you may choose to modify is the elimination period before benefits begin. You may be able to rely on your accumulated wealth to choose a longer elimination period. This will reduce the cost of the policy.

For tax reasons, it is important that you pay 100% of your disability insurance premiums from your after-tax earnings. Otherwise, any future income paid by the policy will be subject to income taxes.

EVALUATE YOUR LIFE INSURANCE COVERAGE

Do not mistake life insurance for an investment product. Many insurance products have an investment vehicle attached to them, but you will almost invariably reap higher returns if you focus on the insurance aspect of your policy and rely on your investment portfolio for wealth growth. The best way to do this is to buy pure term insurance for risk protection and put the premium you save into your investment strategy.

Term Insurance during Your Children's Growing Years

If you have children who have not yet reached adulthood, you will want life insurance to help ensure that they can be raised with the opportunities you have planned. Term life insurance is the simplest and least expensive way to take care of your children and family. Policies are effective for a specified number of years, and they have no cash value at any point in time. If you fail to pay the annual premium, coverage will lapse. Term policies provide a fixed payout that you choose when you purchase the policy.

Many insurance professionals recommend purchasing term insurance in an amount that is a multiple of your current income. However, if you have been quite successful, your income may not reflect the lifestyle you anticipate for you family. I recommend instead that you consider the annual costs of raising your children and maintaining their lifestyle as you would hope. Use this amount to insure a lifestyle for your family.

Protecting the Lifestyle of Your Spouse

If your children have been launched and you're concerned about pre-serving your spouse's lifestyle after you're gone, you may want to additionally consider buying a universal life policy. A universal policy is not as cost effective as term insurance, but it remains in force during your entire lifetime. It often includes an investment-like feature and accumulates a cash value over time. In the situation where you would like to protect a spouse, I recommend starting with a term policy that can be turned into a universal life product in the future.

Forgoing Life Insurance for Now

If you've accumulated sufficient wealth to adequately provide for your loved ones, you may prudently decide to forgo life insurance coverage during certain stages of life. You have insured yourself and your family with your success, and you can instead invest your funds for future growth. Even if you decide to forgo life insurance for risk purposes, you may at some point consider it as a component of your estate planning strategy. Life insurance can be purchased within a trust to provide tax-free wealth transfer to beneficiaries outside of your estate.

PROPERTY RISKS

When did you last check to make sure your home is adequately in-sured? The second category of risks is property risks. If you've lived in your house for some time, you may find that your policy fails to cover improvements you have made, contents you have added, and replace-ment costs that have escalated. Do you have up-to-date coverage for your vacation homes, boats, leisure cars, valuables, and other assets? Your property and casualty coverage is an important component of your risk management, and you should review it with a professional every five to ten years.

It is also a good practice to rethink your policies as your children become teenagers and young adults. When they and their friends begin to stay in the family vacation home, take out the boat, drive your collectible cars, or engage in other activities that create potential liabilities for you, you may want additional coverage.

Unfortunately, as you become increasingly successful, you may become a greater target for property liabilities. If you have not already done so, you may want to consider augmenting your insurance with a personal liability umbrella policy. For a modest cost, it can offer a significant additional level of protection.

INVESTMENT RISKS

We've talked about many different risks to your wealth goals that you can control with insurance. Yet the greatest part of your wealth may be subject to a variety of risks that can't be insured. To assure you reach your goals, you will need to maintain a disciplined commitment to your investment strategy. To do this, it's important to both understand and accept the risks you may encounter in various market environments.

The financial media repeatedly communicates the concept that risk and return are inseparable. What investors most often hear, however, is that higher risk leads to higher returns. They fail to consider that higher risk could potentially lead to personally devastating losses. Professional advisors have spent years refining questionnaires, modeling techniques, and reporting measures, all in an effort to capture and understand clients' financial "risk tolerance." But as seen yet again in 2008, these efforts have repeatedly failed in the real world. One reason for failure, I believe, is the profound disconnect between common measures of risk and investors' personal perceptions of risk.

Discussions of volatility and correlation have cluttered discussions of personal risk. As all investors know, risk is not just a mathematical calculation; it is both the very real possibility of missing your goals and the potentially devastating cost of that failure.

FOUR CATEGORIES OF EXPOSURE TO INVESTMENT RISK

For these reasons, I believe past approaches to discussing portfolio risk have largely outlived their usefulness. To simplify discussions of risk but also make them more meaningful, I find it useful to think about your risk according to the following four types of exposure:

1. Market exposure
2. Opportunistic exposure
3. Specific exposure
4. Capital preservation exposure

Each of these categories describes a different type of investment risk. Ultimately, you will want to feel comfortable with how much of your portfolio is exposed to each of the categories. As you determine your personal risk levels, your investment and asset allocation strategy can naturally flow from your risk exposure decisions.

MARKET EXPOSURE

All marketable investments are exposed to the general, systematic risks inherent in the public markets. In the past, many investors relied on bond investments to balance equity investments in difficult markets. When stocks declined, bonds often outperformed. Similarly, when inflation accelerated, commodities historically protected purchasing power. However, recent data confirms that all publicly traded asset classes in all sectors of the economy and in all geographies are increasingly prone to behave similarly. This means traditional diversification involving different types of asset classes may no longer protect your portfolio in down markets.

Some advisors use computerized models for evaluating potential portfolio risk and allocation among style strategies such as large cap and small cap. While these models are useful tools, they typically start with an assumption that may or may not be true for you. Namely, they assume that you are comfortable exposing all, or substantially all, of your wealth to the uncontrollable volatility of the markets. Since all assets traded in the public markets entail risk, it is essential today to determine first how much of your wealth you feel comfortable exposing to the inevitable ups and downs of any market.

OPPORTUNISTIC EXPOSURE

Next you may want to consider risks that come both from market exposure and individual factors. Opportunistic risk exposure includes investments that are exposed to additional risks due to their unique characteristics. For example, from time to time you may desire to invest in private equity situations, hedge funds, emerging markets, initial public offerings, or high-yield bonds. These are just a few examples of investments that bring opportunistic risk to your portfolio.

At the right price and time, a decision to purchase some of these investments for your portfolio may be appropriate. However, because these higher-risk investments can lose significant value regardless of overall market trends, they belong in a different risk exposure category from your core market investments. For each of your goals, consider whether you are comfortable exposing part of the funds for that goal to opportunistic risk, and reevaluate your decision at regular intervals.

SPECIFIC EXPOSURE

This category relates to the portion of your wealth that is subject to circumstances unique to you. Included in this category are stock options, restricted stock, performance units, or other forms of illiquid compensation granted to you by your employer that are exposed to a significant degree of future uncertainty.

Another common example of specific risk exposure is your privately owned business. A considerable portion of your wealth invariably will be tied to your business, and that wealth may be at risk to economic conditions, competitive pressures, governmental regulations, industry trends, and other factors unique to your business. If your family has large real estate holdings, their value is subject to both interest rate and rental trends. These become specific risks to your wealth. When you evaluate your portfolio and plan your investment strategy, be sure to consider all of these different holdings and their associated risks.

If you have wealth exposed to specific risks, you will want to adjust your exposure to other risk categories that best balance your specific risks.

CAPITAL PRESERVATION EXPOSURE

This category has minimal risk and reflects your wish to maintain principal value. Some investors prefer this level of risk exposure, but assets in this category are unlikely to help your wealth grow toward future goals. If you have accumulated substantial wealth and wish only to maintain the current value of your assets, you might prudently decide to accept only capital preservation risk exposure.

Assets in this category, however, are not risk-free. Even if the amount of your principal is not at risk, the actual value of your principal may lose purchasing power over time due to inflation. If you wish to both preserve your capital and keep pace with future inflation, your portfolio will need some exposure to the market risk category.

Assets within this risk category also tend to produce an income stream, adding an attractive feature for many investors.

RISK CATEGORIES IN PRACTICE

These four categories of risk provide a framework for thinking about your own comfort with investment risk. When you utilize this framework and focus on your goals, you will take the next step toward building your clutter-free wealth plan. Instead of worrying about daily stock market fluctuations, you'll be able to reflect on the investment risks you have carefully embraced.

With each of your goals, consider what risk exposures you are willing to accept. Is the goal already funded? Do you have many years before you hope to achieve the goal? How dependent is the goal on specific risks in your life? When you have considered all these questions, you might add the risk exposure you are comfortable with to your goals chart. Here are the risk exposures Jim and Lisa assigned to their goals we discussed earlier:

Jim and Lisa's Risk Allocations

GOAL	WEALTH	SPECIFIC RISK	MARKET RISK	OPPORT. RISK	CAPITAL PRESERV.
1. College	$0.5M	none	20%	0%	80%
2. Lifestyle	$1.6M	Stock options	60%	10%	30%
3. Parents	$1.1M	none	50%	0%	50%

Jim and Lisa already have accumulated most of the wealth needed to accomplish their education goal, which begins in two years. So while they need to continue to grow the assets to keep up with inflation for their second child, they care most about preserving their existing capital. Though Jim has stock-option exposure, this specific risk has no influence on their education goal.

On the other hand, their long-term lifestyle goal will be highly dependent on the value of Jim's stock-option package. Though it is impossible to value this wealth currently, they determined that the stock options carried risk that was very similar to market risk. So they chose to balance this specific risk with a slightly higher exposure to capital preservation than they might otherwise have chosen. They still have chosen a meaningful exposure to market-related risks, and they are comfortable with the various economic cycles, market fluctuations, and inflation that they may experience to achieve the growth necessary for their goal. Also, they are comfortable with additional opportunistic risk exposure for this goal.

Jim and Lisa have already begun to support their parents. For the next fifteen years, they will need current funds as well as some future growth. To meet this goal, they concluded that they are comfortable with an even split between market risk exposure and capital preservation exposure.

When Jim and Lisa first completed this exercise, we reviewed their allocations relative to their goals. It is a truism in the investment industry that higher risk investments have the potential to earn higher returns. If you find you are most comfortable with the lower risk exposure categories, you may find that it is more difficult to reach your goals. Given the exposures Jim and Lisa chose, we returned to their goals and reconfirmed the likelihood of achieving their goals given the risks with which they felt comfortable.

YOUR TURN

As you carry on with this exercise, notice how it takes you away from traditional ways of looking at investments. Terms such as variance and volatility really just measure the roller coaster ride of your investments. In contrast, this framework helps you truly consider each goal and its importance in your life, taking into account the risks associated with different market exposures. In this way, you can choose a path toward accomplishment that gives you comfort. When you decide on the risk exposures for your goals, you will want to recheck that you still have a high probability of achieving your goals. Once you have confidence in the risk exposures you have embraced, you can complete your chart as Jim and Lisa did:

Jim and Lisa's Risk Allocations

GOAL	WEALTH	SPECIFIC RISK	MARKET RISK	OPPORT. RISK	CAPITAL PRESERV.
1. College	$0.5M	none	20%	0%	80%
2. Lifestyle	$1.6M	Stock options	60%	10%	30%
3. Parents	$1.1M	none	50%	0%	50%
Total	$3.2M		50%	5%	45%

Your completed chart will suggest the risk allocations that you will implement across your total portfolio to achieve your goals. Take a moment to think about the overall risk that your goals suggest. Can you sleep each night with this level of risk exposure? Go back over this process again and again until you are comfortable with the different levels of risk for your goals. Now is the time to adjust your goals if you need less risk exposure.

Next you will use your primary goals and risk exposures to implement a clear and disciplined approach to investing your portfolio.

CHAPTER 7

Aligning Your Investments with Your Goals

Complex investments are not necessarily better. In fact, you can build a simple and effective portfolio that is aligned with your goals and risk exposures. When you track your investment strategy against your wealth goals, you can clearly evaluate your success and weather any market.

Sam, the CEO of a major corporation, and his wife, Anna, had trusted their investments for years to a large, well-known investment management firm. They came to me when Sam retired. Although they had plenty of wealth, they reported that they were uncomfortable with the way their portfolio was performing. Now that Sam was no longer working, they felt they needed more consistent performance to be confident in their goals.

Sam and Anna reported that they were ready to enjoy their lifestyle. They also wanted to fund the education of all their grandchildren, and they wanted to start thinking about a legacy for the long run. With the wealth they had accumulated, all of these goals were very achievable.

When we began to discuss their current investment portfolio, Sam shared plenty of data as the firm produced a report for him and Anna every quarter that was over 100 pages long and a half-inch thick. As we reviewed it together, I noticed that they had a number of more complex investments such as hedge funds, illiquid holdings in private company stock, structured investments, and many different fund vehicles. The performance of each investment was also reported, and the total portfolio performance was reported and compared to a custom benchmark provided by the advisor. Despite all this data and reporting, Sam and Anna did not know if their portfolio was meeting their goals.

We went through the process of determining how much market exposure they felt comfortable with. We talked about their specific risk exposure, which included a privately held company with which Sam was involved, and we discussed where principal protection made the most sense.

It did not take long for all of us to come to the conclusion that a much simpler, more predictable, and more understandable portfolio would give them the confidence that they could accomplish all their goals.

BUILDING AN EFFECTIVE YET SIMPLE PORTFOLIO

When you are clear about your goals and your comfort levels, it becomes much easier to choose the most appropriate investments for your portfolio. Many people think that for peak performance, the complexity of their portfolio should increase as their wealth increases. I emphatically disagree.

When you focus on building a portfolio that pursues your goals, a well-planned allocation to equities, fixed income, and cash can be effective. It may not provide interesting party conversation, but you are more likely to master your investments and be able to judge your portfolio's success toward your goals.

THE CORE AND SATELLITE APPROACH

I like to use what I call the core and satellite approach for building a portfolio. Graphically, this approach looks like a hub with spokes. The hub represents your market exposure and principal protection investments. You can have a very successful portfolio with just this core, and many people do.

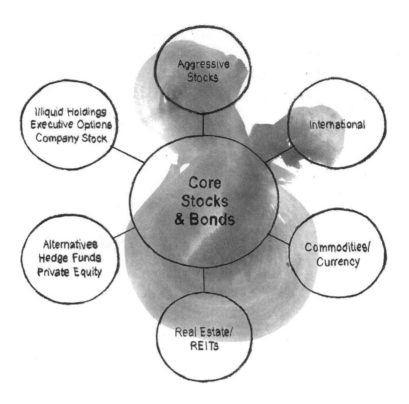

Your satellite investments around the hub consist of investments with opportunistic risk and specific risk. If you own a family business, that satellite might actually be as big or bigger than your core, while other satellites with opportunistic risk may be quite small, reflecting the disproportionate risk outside your core.

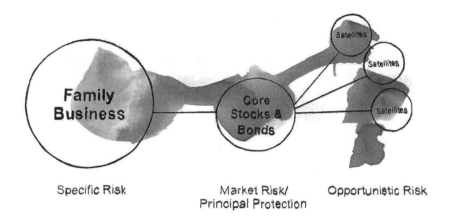

| Specific Risk | Market Risk/
Principal Protection | Opportunistic Risk |

With this framework in mind, we're ready to start allocating investments to your goals.

INVESTING FOR YOUR GOALS

After you've established your wealth requirements for each goal, you are ready to allocate investments. Most people, including many investment advisors, begin by selecting core investments. These are your market exposure and principal protection assets. In fact, many advisors ignore specific risk investments entirely. This is a big mistake. The best place to start is with your specific risk assets, those assets such as a family business or employee options that are subject to circumstances unique to you. When these very important assets are allocated first, you can take them into account when you are choosing your core investments.

For example, if your wealth carries specific risk from a deferred compensation package that promises to generate a sizable stream of income in the future, you would want to keep that in mind as you select market exposure and principal protection investments. Likewise, you would probably want to balance an asset that has high specific risk exposure, such as ownership of a technology start-up company with core investments that are more predictable.

For example, Neil is an executive in a financial services firm. A significant portion of his total wealth is tied to a deferred compensation plan and options holdings, small amounts of which will come due annually starting several years in the future. On any given day, we can estimate what the value of this compensation may be, but the level of uncertainty will be high for some time to come. It was important for us to take this uncertainty into account when building the rest of his portfolio. When we then moved on to the core portfolio, we decided that we would intentionally avoid investments in the financial services industry, since both his professional career and so much of his future wealth were derived from it. This was a very important decision that significantly protected his total wealth in 2008. Though his professional life felt very precarious during that time, he was relieved to know that the rest of his wealth was protected from the same exposure. This is just one example that illustrates why it is best to evaluate specific risks first, and then build the rest of your portfolio around them.

Once you have allocated your specific risk assets to your various goals, you can continue the process by choosing appropriate core investments from the market exposure and principal protection categories.

MARKET EXPOSURE INVESTMENTS

When considering market exposure investments, you will most likely choose from fund vehicles or individual stocks. If you are comfortable with the rollercoaster of the broader market, you might choose to use funds that mimic a broad stock market index. These are generally described as passive investments in that a professional is not actively building a portfolio of stocks for you. Passive index investments are very cost effective.

If you are looking for market exposure that balances a specific risk of yours or that does not follow the roller coaster of the broader market, you will probably prefer an actively managed portfolio. Your financial advisor may build a portfolio of individual stocks for you or perhaps recommend an experienced manager to invest this part of your core portfolio. This approach can fit your needs better and offer more personalized tax management.

PRINCIPAL PROTECTION INVESTMENTS

Numerous fixed income securities, most commonly bonds, are available to provide capital protection and different levels of taxable or tax-free income. For your principal protection allocation, you probably do not want fixed income funds. Once a principal protection asset is put into a fund, the principal is no longer assured. For example, when you buy a single bond of a financially sound company, no matter how the market fluctuates, at maturity you will receive the full principal value of the bond. When you buy a fixed income fund, the many different bonds in the fund change value daily. There is no set date on which you receive your principal back. In fact, within a fund, bonds are often regularly traded so that even a single bond may not be held to maturity. You do not want these kinds of investments for principal protection. Instead, purchase individual bonds to provide principal protection exposure.

It is best to use a professional advisor to help you select individual fixed income investments. Fixed income investments vary by maturity and credit quality. A U.S. Treasury bond is considered the safest investment you can choose, with the highest credit quality available. The longer the maturity of the Treasury bond you purchase, the higher interest rate you will be paid on the bond. That is, you want to be rewarded for tying up your investment for a longer time frame. A corporate bond sold by General Electric or AT&T, for example, will offer a slightly higher interest rate compared to a U.S. Treasury bond of the same maturity. The higher interest rate reflects the difference in credit quality between the U.S. government and a corporation. You will want to adjust the mix of maturities and credit quality of your investments to provide the principal protection you seek to achieve your goals.

These two categories complete your core investments. Many wealthy families achieve all of their goals with a core investment portfolio. Like them, you may find it appealing to have a simple, yet effective approach.

OPPORTUNISTIC EXPOSURE

Depending on your needs and tolerance for risk, you might add some satellite opportunistic investments. As we discussed earlier, these investments may be appropriate for your goals at different times. Depending on the investment, you may utilize funds, individual securities, or derivative structures.

I suggest your opportunistic investments should all pass the "mother test": if you cannot explain the investment to your mother, avoid it. As we discussed at the outset, higher complexity does not ensure more attractive returns. What it does ensure is that you will quickly lose confidence in the investment if the value temporarily drops and you do not understand it thoroughly enough to maintain your investment discipline. Instead of focusing on how your total is moving toward your goals, you will tend to focus on a single investment. If this occurs, you will know that your investment strategy has gone off course.

EXECUTING YOUR STRATEGY

Now that you have a general idea about how to build your investment portfolio, how do you actually execute your strategy? If you find this process confusing, be sure to work closely with your professional financial advisor. You may, in fact, prefer to have an advisor that can take care of the day-to-day investing for you.

INVESTING SUCCESSFULLY UNDER PROFESSIONAL COMPLIANCE GUIDELINES

I have met a number of successful executives who believe that their profession prohibits them from benefiting from the day-to-day execution of a professional advisor. They think they may only own diversified mutual fund vehicles that rarely meet their personal investment allocations. A number of professions, such as financial services and law, impose strict compliance guidelines on securities trading to avoid conflicts of interest and the dissemination of insider information. Even under these policies, most executives can take advantage of personalized professional investment management.

Many compliance areas can accept a letter from the executive and investment manager confirming that they are entering a fully discretionary relationship in which the investment manager will make the day-to-day decisions regarding individual securities trading. When this approach is not sufficient, an executive can usually create a blind trust. This is a legal trust in which the investment advisor, as a fiduciary, is given full discretion to make daily investment decisions on behalf of the trust beneficiary. It takes a compliance letter to the level of a formal legal structure.

GOING IT ALONE

Some people choose to handle the investment process themselves. If you prefer to execute investment strategy yourself, a multitude of resources are available on the Internet and from discount brokerage firms to help you identify investments that match your needs and your risk/comfort profile. Many also offer information and encouragement about how to manage your own portfolio.

Before you decide to be your own money manager, however, it's helpful to understand your motivation. Some people find satisfaction and enjoyment in handling their own financial affairs and have ample time for it. If that describes you, this might be a good option. Other people choose to manage their own money because they don't want to incur the expense of a professional advisor. That's usually not a good motivation, because the investment you make in a competent, experienced professional almost always will more than pay for itself. Remember, a professional advisor has the training and experience to design your personal portfolio strategy. Additionally, a professional advisor spends every day, full-time, overseeing investment portfolios.

If you decide to manage your own portfolio, be sure to set aside regular time for research and record keeping. You may not need to spend time on your investments every day, but you do need to stay on top of things so that you can adjust to any important changes in your own circumstances, in your portfolio, and in the general market.

When you're on your own, it's sometimes difficult to measure how well you're tracking with your goals. Although discount brokerages usually report on how each position has performed in relation to cost, they typically don't provide portfolio-level performance data and internal rates of return.

Personal finance software will allow you to track the cost basis of your portfolio, and some of the online vendors will do that as well. But be forewarned that these programs generally don't handle performance calculations very well. For instance, when securities split or merge, or when dividends are reinvested, the popular retail programs may not be able to provide a true internal rate of return on the investment.

ASSESSING YOUR PROGRESS

You are likely to find that you can be very disciplined about sticking to your investment approach now that it is aligned with your values and your goals. You won't be overly concerned about how well an individual investment performed in the last quarter, or exactly how you should invest your next bonus. Rather, you'll be asking such questions as, "How am I doing compared to my overall goals? Have I moved closer to them? Does this progress or lack of progress warrant a change in my investment strategy? Has anything changed in my life that prompts me to refine or change my objectives?"

Although you'll want to assess your portfolio regularly and you'll be interested in how the broad market averages fluctuate, you'll be a lot more interested in how your portfolio performs compared to your goals. When you review quarterly or annual portfolio performance, you'll want to compare that performance on an annualized basis to the returns you determined were necessary to achieve your goals.

UNDERSTANDING INVESTMENT RETURNS

It's not easy to assess annualized returns because many different advisors, software programs, and Internet sites report returns differently. The most common of the confusing measures are the following:

- Price return
- Total return
- Return compared to cost
- Time-weighted total return

PRICE RETURN

This popular measure of return reports how the price of the investment has changed. You might think that this is exactly what is important to you. However, many investments also pay dividends or interest, and these cash payments are part of the return on your investment. If you only look at the cost of your portfolio compared to the ending value, you may be missing any income you have been withdrawing. Most often, when the financial media report the returns of a market average, they're talking about the price return. This is one reason why many financial advisors caution against comparing your portfolio to a market index.

TOTAL RETURN

Total return is the correct way to think about the appreciation in your investment portfolio. It is the combination of the capital appreciation in your investments as well as the income produced by the investments. Often when I meet with people who will be living off their assets, they focus solely on the income produced by the portfolio. I explain to them that their lifestyle is supported by the total return of their portfolio.

RETURN COMPARED TO COST

Many brokerage reports and Internet sites report returns on individual securities compared to cost. As each year goes by, that performance measure becomes increasingly dominated by returns of the distant past. The investment might actually be down on the year or the quarter, but still up compared to the original cost. Also, you may have made several purchases at different times, but the return on cost cannot take this in consideration. While it may be interesting to know how the investment has performed since it was purchased, in the investment profession we like to say, "cost is as important as yesterday's news." Once you have made the investment, you will be interested in the annual growth toward your goal. An annualized return calculation moves past cost and takes your return since purchase and adjusts it to report what has been your success on a yearly basis.

TIME-WEIGHTED TOTAL RETURN

The standard that you will want to use is known as time-weighted total returns. This calculation, sometimes also known as the internal rate of return on your investments, overcomes all of the shortcomings mentioned above. It combines both your capital appreciation and your income returns, and it takes into consideration the timing of all your purchases and sales.

Once you are sure you are receiving appropriate return measures, you will want to compare these returns over time to your overall return goal. I find this much easier to do visually, and I like to show clients a chart that starts with the opening value of their portfolio and follows their "goal path" over time.

Achieving Long-term Goals

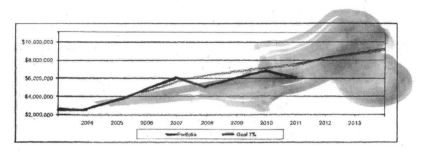

This sample only reflects annual changes in the portfolio value. It is best not to judge your progress quarter to quarter—or even on a year-to-year basis—but over a full market cycle.

Historically, a full market cycle lasts anywhere from three to five years. Within that period there is likely to be considerable volatility, so assessing performance on less than a full cycle can produce misleading results. You'll get a better idea about how well your portfolio is performing by capturing a full cycle of ups and downs.

In the recession of 2008, for example, it's not surprising that investors who attempted to measure their progress quarterly or annually became quite discouraged. But since most of my clients had been tracking portfolio performance for a few years prior, they were able to see that at various times they had been above or below the path toward their goals. Although they were now below the path, their past experience with the goals approach gave them confidence that their portfolios would recover on the path to their goals and they were still likely to achieve the results they desired in the time frames they had specified.

You, too, are likely to find that when you are deliberate about implementing an investment strategy toward your goals, you won't be easily enticed by the latest fads in the financial media or scared by the latest market volatility. You will be both financially and emotionally invested in your strategy, and you will be able to maintain your investment discipline with confidence.

CHAPTER 8

Refining Your Asset Location Strategy

Unlike institutional investors, your portfolio is subject to taxes and withdrawals. Using asset location strategies, each of your accounts plays a different role in your portfolio. This approach can meaningfully improve your after-tax success.

Often clients come to me after reading about the latest strategies of the Yale Endowment and other well-known institutions, and they ask, "How much wealth do I need before I can be managed like that?"

"You're not an institution," I tell them, "and it would be a mistake to try to imitate one. Institutional endowments don't have to pay taxes, and they have only one account. Their investment strategies assume an endless time horizon, and their withdrawals typically are scheduled well in advance to meet predictable liability obligations."

Individuals have to take into consideration many more variables. Even if you have simplified your financial affairs, it is likely that you have a taxable investment account or two, a deferred retirement account such as an IRA or Roth IRA, and perhaps one or more trust accounts. More importantly, you must pay taxes; you need to withdraw funds for a variety of needs at irregular intervals; and you need to take into account multiple time horizons.

No wonder so many individual investors feel envious when they read about endowment funds! But all of these different variables also present you with some attractive opportunities. The key is to know how to locate your assets in the most efficient accounts.

MANY ADVISORS IGNORE ASSET LOCATION

Jake and Beth came to me for advice because they were unhappy with the counsel they had been receiving from their previous financial advisor. As I looked over their portfolio, I noticed that Beth's accounts were virtually a mirror image of her husband's. In each of their accounts they had exactly the same investments: 1000 shares of IBM in his, 1000 shares of IBM in hers, and so on. Unfortunately, this type of inefficient portfolio is very common. Such duplication needlessly increases costs and complexity, without reducing risks. Merely placing the same investments in different accounts is not diversification.

Instead of striving for symmetry, I advise all of my clients to consider each of their accounts as a piece of the big picture. Every investment should play its own role in the most efficient account, without regard to mirroring other accounts. The practice of locating investments to their best advantage is known as asset location.

Recent research indicates that adding purposeful asset location strategies to portfolios can increase investment returns by a half percent or more. Over time, this can amount to a substantial amount of money.

DIFFERENT ACCOUNTS FOR DIFFERENT INVESTMENTS

Each of your accounts can be used to your advantage for different investments. Unfortunately, there is not an exact strategy for everyone, as the best location for your assets varies by a number of factors such as your:

- Tax situation
- Time horizon
- Need for income withdrawals
- Other personal circumstances

Developing a sound asset location strategy can also be a challenge because tax laws are always subject to change. In the current environment, uncertainty about future tax rates is especially high. For this reason, always confirm your personal tax situation with your accountant.

TAXABLE TRANSACTIONS

Generally speaking, there are three types of taxable transactions that can occur in your accounts:

- Capital gains and losses
- Interest income
- Dividend income

CAPITAL GAINS AND LOSSES

The sale of an investment asset will result in a capital gain when the proceeds of the sale exceed the original cost of the investment. If the asset is located in your individual taxable account, you will incur a tax liability for the amount of the capital gain. Currently capital gains are taxed at either 15% or 0%, depending on your income level.

If the proceeds of the sale of an asset amount to less than the original cost of the investment, the difference will result in a capital loss. You are allowed to use your losses to offset capital gains in the current year, and you can additionally report up to $3,000 in losses beyond that. Any unapplied tax loss from the current year may be carried forward and used to offset capital gains in future years.

INTEREST INCOME

Interest income paid on money market funds or bonds is subject to taxes at your ordinary income tax rate. Therefore, you will usually want to avoid placing interest-paying investments in a taxable account.

DIVIDEND INCOME

Dividend income may be qualified or non-qualified. Qualified dividend income is taxed up to 15%. At this low rate, these assets may be appropriate for a taxable account. The IRS code provides detailed criteria for determining whether dividends are qualified. For example, the dividend must be paid by a corporation that is regularly traded on a U.S. stock exchange, and you must own the shares more than 60 days in any 120-day period.

ACCOUNT STRUCTURE

Your tax location strategy is influenced by both the taxable nature of transactions as well as the structure of your account. Typical account structures include the following:

- Taxable accounts
- Tax-deferred accounts
- Tax-free retirement accounts
- Trust accounts with varying tax status

TAXABLE ACCOUNTS

If you're like most investors, you probably have one or more personal investment accounts that are subject to taxation. In a taxable personal account, capital gains are currently taxed at relatively low rates, and capital losses have some value because they can be used to offset gains. In our current tax environment, even the highest income earners are subject to only 15% taxes on capital gains. At this low rate, a taxable account can be a good place to put quality growth assets. Both the qualified dividends and investment profits generated in these accounts will be taxed at this low rate. Generally speaking, it would be unwise to put corporate bonds that pay interest or non-qualified preferred stock in this type of account, since the income would be subject to taxes at your ordinary income tax rate.

There is a good exception to this guidance, however. If your taxable investment account is very small relative to any tax-deferred retirement accounts you have, it may make sense to utilize the taxable account entirely for investments in tax-free municipal bonds. The bonds will offer capital protection, and the income they generate will be tax-free.

TAX-DEFERRED ACCOUNTS

In addition to a personal taxable account, you probably have one or more traditional retirement accounts. These might include IRAs, 401(k)s, 403(b)s, or maybe a self-employed retirement plan such as a SEP or a solo 401(k). For purposes of discussion, I'll lump all of these under the general heading of tax-deferred accounts.

Tax-deferred means that you will not have to pay taxes on the income generated in these accounts until you withdraw it. Under current law, you may begin taking distributions after age fifty-five, and you are required to begin taking distributions in the year you turn 70 1/2 or the year after. At that time, distributions will be taxed at your ordinary income tax rate.

A big advantage of tax-deferred accounts is that interest income, dividend income, and capital gains in the account can be reinvested, and the appreciation will be tax-free. One disadvantage of tax-deferred accounts, however, is that capital losses cannot be used to offset realized gains on your annual income taxes.

Capital Preservation in Your Tax-Deferred Accounts

Because tax-deferred accounts postpone taxation, sometimes for many years, they can be a great location for investments that generate taxable income, such as corporate bond interest or real estate investment trust distributions. All income generated by the assets will be tax-free until distribution.

Since these accounts are usually meant to fund a future retirement lifestyle, you might appreciate investments that are more reliable and will maintain their value in volatile markets. In assigning the bulk of your capital protection risk exposure to tax-deferred accounts, you defer the taxes on the interest income and also ensure more stable value for your accounts.

My clients, Katherine and John, have done a great job using this strategy. They are far along in their careers, and they plan to leave their primary occupations before too long. I advised them to allocate some bonds into their tax-deferred retirement accounts to provide principal protection in the event of an economic downturn. This is an efficient way to safeguard their long-term retirement goals, since the interest income generated by these bonds will be tax-free and can be reinvested for future growth.

Tax-deferred Accounts for More Aggressive Growth

Occasionally a different approach is warranted. Let me tell you about two young executives I work with who have a good reason to think about their deferred accounts differently. Scott and Andrew already have accumulated substantial wealth, and they both plan to continue working for a good number of years. Because they have a very long time horizon before they will be forced to make withdrawals from their retirement accounts, they are comfortable with the volatility that comes with aggressive investments. In this case, their tax-deferred accounts will allow for more frequent trading and large appreciation potential over the many years without generating any capital gain taxes.

If you have a similar situation, you might consider relocating some of your more aggressive assets into your tax-deferred accounts to shield their capital gains from taxation. Of course, if the investments generate losses, you will not be able to use these losses to offset taxable gains in other accounts.

TAX-FREE RETIREMENT ACCOUNTS

Roth IRAs, Roth 401(k)s, or Roth 403(b)s, like traditional retirement accounts, allow investments and income to be paid and reinvested tax-free. But unlike a traditional retirement account, current law allows for tax-free distributions from these accounts. Furthermore, you never are required to take distributions. For this reason, Roth accounts are attractive for investments with very long-term time horizons such as aggressive and illiquid equity investments.

TRUSTS ACCOUNTS

Many successful families utilize various types of irrevocable trusts to help achieve their estate planning goals. Because trusts are subject to different tax treatments depending on their terms, thoughtful consideration should be given to the selection and placement of assets. Make these decisions on a case-by-case basis in coordination with your investment advisor and accountant, taking into account your personal tax considerations, your time horizon, and your investment asset-location plan.

Charitable trusts and foundations can be an attractive way to transfer wealth to charities. Even though the charity will actually own the assets, the investor can maintain substantial control by determining a preferred investment strategy that is consistent with the goals of the charitable beneficiary. Investments within the trust can be traded tax-free, making these trusts an ideal location for donations of highly appreciated stock you already own. Once donated to the charitable trust, the shares can be sold without generating any capital gains tax. Depending on the structure of the account, you may be taxed on income or distributions, so it is important to be very familiar with the trust structure you choose.

Here is a table that briefly summarizes how the transactions are treated in different kinds of accounts you might own:

Summary of Asset Location

ACCOUNT STRUCTURE	CAPITAL GAINS	INTEREST INCOME	DIVIDENDS	WITHDRAWALS
Taxable Investment Account	Taxable	Taxable	Taxable	Tax-Free
Tax-Deferred Account	Tax-Free	Tax-Free	Tax-Free	Taxable
Tax-Free Account	Tax-Free	Tax-Free	Tax-Free	Tax-Free
Trust Account	Varies	Varies	Varies	Tax-Free

ASSET LOCATION AS AN OPPORTUNITY

Determining asset location is an important step in the investment process. Although it may seem challenging, it also provides some unique opportunities at certain times, such as when tax laws change. Tim took advantage of such an opportunity when the tax laws were recently changed to allow high-income earners to convert traditional IRAs to Roth IRAs.

Tim had a sizable IRA that represented about 20% of his wealth. He had been keeping a variety of taxable corporate and government bonds in this IRA, which allowed him to defer income taxes on the interest they generated. His long-term goal is to pass these assets down through several generations.

As we reviewed his investment and estate plans, I suggested that he could benefit from an IRA conversion. By converting his traditional IRA to a Roth IRA, he could more easily achieve his legacy goal because he would avoid the requirement to withdraw money from his IRA when he reached 70½ years of age.

Since this Roth account would have a very long time horizon and would be part of his legacy planning to benefit future generations, I proposed that he use the funds in this account for some of his most aggressive investments. Although some of these investments might lose money in the short term, over the long term they were likely to appreciate. As he sold and purchased investments, the Roth IRA would shield all gains from taxes, so he would be able to reinvest the entire proceeds.

THE FINAL CLUTTER IN YOUR INVESTMENT PORTFOLIO

By strategically locating your investment assets, you will eliminate the last of the clutter in your portfolio. Your investment strategy should reflect your overall goals, and each account should reflect a clear tactical strategy. Securities will no longer mirror each other across accounts, and you will be able to monitor the tax efficiency of each account as part of the whole. Once this is done, you will be ready to attack the clutter in the other critical areas of your wealth plan.

CHAPTER 9

Thinking about Your Legacy

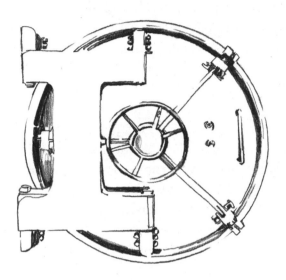

Estate planning should begin either as you start to accumulate wealth or when you start a family. There are only four steps to a basic clutter-free estate plan. But life is always changing, so it is important for you to review your plans at least every five years.

When I work with people who have just had their first child, I tell them, "Congratulations on the arrival of your new daughter! Now, let's update your will so that it clearly specifies who will care for your child in your absence and what resources will be available for her care."

Your guardianship provisions for underage children are among the most important aspects of your will. This is just one of the reasons why you shouldn't wait until you retire to begin your legacy planning. Laying the groundwork for your legacy goals starts when you have family, significant assets, or both.

I'm shocked at how many families with substantial means have never put together even a basic estate plan. When I ask some of them what has held them back, they usually reply that they are so overwhelmed by what they hear in the news and read in books about the ever changing tax laws for estates that they become paralyzed. Some of them have even met with an estate attorney, but have not followed through on the recommendations because they were given a laundry list of tasks to complete. They decided, "I don't have time to go through all these steps. I'll worry about my estate another day."

A SIMPLE FOUR-STEP ESTATE PLAN

Estate planning is about taking care of yourself and others in the event the unexpected occurs.

Estate planning is too important to be ignored or postponed, and it need not be overwhelming. Indeed, a full and complete estate plan can have many pieces, but that is refinement that appropriately builds over many years. You can start an effective, clutter-free estate plan by following this simple four-step process:

1. Prepare your will.
2. Prepare your advance directive.
3. Title your assets and designate your beneficiaries.
4. Organize your vital records.

PREPARE YOUR WILL

If you pass away without a will, the court steps in and distributes your assets according to the laws of your state and determines who will serve as guardian of your children. Your last will and testament is a legal directive that provides for the care of your family, instructs how to allocate your assets, and appoints an executor to administer your wishes. It can also communicate your important wishes to others. Your will requires your notarized signature, and depending on your state, a number of witnesses as well. However, a beneficiary of your will cannot sign as a witness.

Your first important decision in your will may be to name a guardian for your children. Families with significant assets often name both a care guardian and a financial guardian, separating the roles of raising children from managing their money. This creates oversight to ensure funds are used appropriately for your children's care and well being. You may want to name successor guardians in case your first choice is not available. Also, remember that you may need to revisit this decision over time. Your closest friends and relatives when your children are born may be living in Singapore ten years later.

Next, you will need to name an executor for your will. The executor manages your estate from the time of your death until your assets are fully distributed. An executor's duties include identifying all your assets, paying any creditors, filing estate taxes, and making sure your wishes are carried out. This is an important task, and an executor's job may last a few months to several years. Therefore, you may choose to name more than one executor and a couple of contingent executors.

Now you are ready to consider the distribution of your assets. Start with your wealth inventory to be sure you consider all your assets. Depending on your wealth, your assets may pass to your spouse, your children, or a variety of trusts that more specifically achieve your desires. Many estate planners can offer a variety of strategies for distributing your assets while minimizing taxes. You might find some of these ideas helpful, but don't let your tax-avoidance tactics become so complex that you lose the ease and comfort of a well-crafted plan. A properly executed will eliminates confusion and relieves you and your heirs of undue stress.

When preparing your will, enlist the services of a qualified estate-planning attorney. Your attorney will know the most recent governing laws and help you think through short-term and long-term issues. He or she will evaluate your unique circumstances so that the document you create will accomplish your goals while helping you avoid costly mistakes. Over the years, you should regularly revisit your will to adjust for changes in your life, your wealth, and prevailing tax and estate laws.

PREPARE YOUR ADVANCE DIRECTIVE

The second essential document is the advance directive, which informs family and health care professionals about your end-of-life wishes. Typically this document will not be necessary until you are quite old, but as soon as you are twenty-one, you should prepare an advance directive. Also called a living will, a durable power of attorney, or a health care proxy, your advance directive essentially is an incapacity plan. This extremely important document authorizes a person, legally called your agent, to make health care decisions on your behalf, in the event you are medically incapacitated.

Take care to choose the right person as your agent, and consider appointing a contingent agent in case your primary designee is unavailable. Also, you may want to consider putting certain limitations on your authorizations. For instance, your advance directive might specify that your agent can make decisions on your behalf only after you have been incapacitated for a certain amount of time or based on a likely prognosis from a medical professional.

When you look at an advance directive, you will notice that it mentions HIPAA (the Health Information Portability and Accountability Act), which is the federal law governing the disclosure of private health care information. In compliance with HIPAA, your advance directive should stipulate when and to whom you will allow disclosure of your protected information.

You may already have a basic advance directive that you haven't thought much about. If you have ever been admitted to a hospital or other health care institution, it is likely that you were offered some sort of generic advance directive when you checked in. It may have been applied only to that stay, or you may have kept a copy for enduring power.

Your estate-planning attorney will have a more thorough document for you to customize, and he or she will help you consider the critical issues. However, do not complete any forms until you have considered your decisions in consultation with the important people around you. Unfortunately, misunderstanding and even abuse can arise when it comes to incapacity issues. So make sure your advance directive clearly states your desires, and of course, make sure the appropriate people know where to find it when they need it.

TITLE YOUR ASSETS AND DESIGNATE YOUR BENEFICIARIES

You will now have completed two of the most important steps to your estate plan. The next step is to make sure that the rest of your life is properly aligned with the decisions you have made so far. The most carefully planned will is useless if you independently have named beneficiaries and joint owners for your assets that contradict the wishes in your will.

Perhaps in the past, you purchased life insurance, opened an IRA or 401(k) retirement plan, or participated in a profit-sharing or pension plan. The odds are high that you named beneficiaries on the original documents. If you were single, perhaps the beneficiary was another family member. If you were just starting out in a marriage, you may have named your spouse. If you left that form blank years ago, most states specify by default that the beneficiary is your spouse.

Now is the time to review and update all of these designations. In most instances, you will want to add contingent beneficiaries to certain assets. This option offers your beneficiaries greater flexibility in managing your assets. If desired, they can disclaim an asset and allow it to pass to a contingent beneficiary that might be more appropriate. For example, you may determine that for tax and wealth-transfer purposes you should name your children or grandchildren as contingent beneficiaries after your spouse. You also may find it advantageous to name a trust as the beneficiary of your life insurance policies, retirement plans, or other assets. The beneficiary listed on each asset will take precedence over your will, so take the time to be thorough, specific, and accurate. Improper designations on any of your assets can ruin the best estate plans.

Next review the ownership titles to all of your assets. This includes savings accounts and investment accounts, of course, as well as your homes, boats, investment real estate, and automobiles. Perhaps when you purchased these assets, you decided on the spur of the moment to own them with your spouse as joint tenants with rights of survivorship. This is the most common choice for spouses and sometimes for parents and children as well. It allows for immediate and full transfer to the surviving joint owner. However, if you have made specific decisions in your will, or if you want to take advantage of estate tax exclusions for your spouse, this default choice may contradict your goals. Other appropriate ownership choices may include sole ownership, tenants-in-common, or designated beneficiary/transfer-on-death titling. Each of these options has specific advantages depending on your estate plans.

So be sure to ask about the appropriate titles for all your holdings as you make plans with your estate-planning attorney.

ORGANIZE YOUR VITAL RECORDS

Once you've done all this work, the worst thing you can do is file these documents away in the back of the closet! It is critical that the important people in your life know where to find your important documents. It is so important, in fact, that I consider this the fourth step in your clutter-free estate plan.

In the event of your incapacity or death, the people in your life need to know where to find your will, titles, policies, and other vital records. They will also need to know the names and addresses of your advisors, the passwords to your various accounts, and the location of your safe deposit boxes.

For this reason, I strongly recommend that you record all of the above information in a vital records organizer. Keep this information where it can be readily accessed in an emergency. If you name a trust company or lawyer as your executor, they will keep a copy. You might think to keep this information in your safe deposit box, but you should know that some states seal your safe deposit box upon your death. So many people decide to keep their vital records organizer in a desk drawer file, on a labeled CD, or in a secure computer file.

Most attorneys have a vital records template you can use to help ensure that you don't overlook anything. I've also included a sample organizer in Appendix B and on our website.

Start with the wealth inventory you created because it already includes much of the information you will need for your vital records organizer. Then update the document from time to time so that it remains relevant. Having this information in one place will give you and your loved ones greater peace of mind, and it will help ensure that the estate plan you've worked so hard to prepare will be effectively carried out.

KEEPING IT CLUTTER-FREE

Your estate planning is like refilling your wardrobe in a cleaned-out closet. First you add a few of the basics to get you through each day. That's what we've done here. In four easy steps you and your family will have basic protection and plans. As you get comfortable with the look in your new wardrobe, you will have the energy to go back and consider more additions—a few more accessories. As you think about your estate plan over time, you may "accessorize" with specific-purpose trusts that help you distribute your assets even more purposefully and reduce the potential taxes on your estate. Like filling in the closet, these enhancements can be added gradually over time. Finally, just as your wardrobe can go stale, refresh your estate plan every three to five years. Update it immediately when there are any major changes in your life or that of your family.

CHAPTER 10

Giving to Make a Difference

Charitable commitments enrich your life in many ways. Thinking about your philanthropy strategically will free you from constant check writing and help you achieve even more satisfaction. Embracing the causes that bring you meaning can even improve your legacy plans.

Americans are the most charitable people in the world. Regardless of level of income, we generously give both time and money to public and private organizations of all kinds. When there is a natural disaster or a great need, the world always looks to America for support. We are committed to giving because we find it enriching on so many levels.

PHILANTHROPY AS A RESPONSIBILITY OF SUCCESS

Some people give because they feel a social imperative. They consider their own financial success in comparison to the ills in our society, and they feel a duty to give back. In supporting charities that touch them or feel meaningful, these donors find personal satisfaction and perhaps a sense of balance with their wealth.

PHILANTHROPY TO BUILD FAMILY COHESION

For some, supporting charitable priorities together can promote family cohesion and communicate shared values for future generations. Some families have found that their work with charitable organizations has also provided educational opportunities for their children to learn leadership and financial skills. More and more families are also embracing Andrew Carnegie's view, "The parent who leaves his son enormous wealth generally deadens the talents and energies of the son." These families prefer to involve their families in lasting philanthropic commitments for their wealth, rather than pass the bulk to future generations.

PHILANTHROPY TO EXTEND NETWORKS AND CAREERS

Commitments of both money and personal time to philanthropic organizations can also connect like-minded people. Professionals who are responsible for business development often choose to support organizations and become involved in their board leadership. These individuals not only are supporting worthy causes, but their devotion of time allows them to work with other interesting and successful people who can extend their personal and professional networks.

PHILANTHROPY FOR A PRACTICAL LEGACY

There are also legacy reasons to pursue philanthropic ventures. Many people have the means to work with a charitable organization to create a truly memorable legacy in one's community. Committing their wealth to a major capital project allows these donors to see their life's accomplishments support an ongoing purpose. It also allows these donors to define how they will be remembered. On a more practical note, if an individual dies with a taxable estate, the U.S. government decides how the taxes will be spent in our society. Some people prefer to make their own decisions as to how their wealth will be reinvested in our society. Therefore, they employ charitable commitments in their estate planning to reduce the size of their taxable estate.

These are all good reasons to explore philanthropic opportunities. In my experience, most prosperous people want to support charitable endeavors, yet they often get bogged down in finding the most effective approach to their goals. Like their investments, they accumulate philanthropic clutter. Yes, there is a clutter-free approach to philanthropy that can productively support the causes you care about, involve your family, and improve your estate plan. With this approach, I have seen philanthropy develop into the number one wealth priority for a number of successful people.

THE MOST COMMON APPROACH TO CHARITABLE GIVING

The most common approach to charitable giving is what I call "checkbook philanthropy." Checkbook philanthropists sit down once a year, and sometimes more often, and write checks for the charities important to them. This approach is very straightforward and the one I most often see with new clients. By writing lots of checks, you spread your support across many worthy causes. Over time, you probably add a few more causes that seem worthy, and periodically you sit with the whole list and consider which charities might receive higher contributions as your personal success grows. At tax time, you search for a growing list of receipts and confirmation letters to send to your accountant.

The clutter-free alternative is often called strategic philanthropy. This approach can amplify your charitable impact while reducing the clutter in your tax files. Strategic philanthropists search their personal values and priorities to help them proactively identify worthwhile causes. Then they develop giving plans with specific goals to fund them. As they periodically review their activities in light of their goals, they might tend to single out fewer charities for meaningful support.

FOUR CATEGORIES OF STRATEGIC PHILANTHROPY

While this concept sounds appealing, you may be trying to consider how you move from your current approach to a strategic approach. Strategic philanthropists tend to fall into one of several categories that reflect the way they involve themselves in organizations:

1. The responsive philanthropist
2. The investing philanthropist
3. The problem-solving philanthropist
4. The social philanthropist

If you can place yourself in one of these support styles, it will help you move forward with a purposeful approach to your philanthropy.

THE RESPONSIVE PHILANTHROPIST

Perhaps you like to respond to specific needs as they come to your attention. When you learn about a need from an appeal letter or from a solicitation phone call that fits within your predetermined strategic parameters, you often make a one-time donation. This approach can deliver meaningful support at times of critical need or funding shortfalls. As a responsive philanthropist, you are strategic with your financial gifts. This approach is often appealing to very busy people who want to make a difference, but who do not have the time to involve themselves more personally in causes.

THE INVESTING PHILANTHROPIST

Instead of waiting for appeals from charities, perhaps you are an investing philanthropist. You prefer to proactively look for causes aligned with your charitable priorities and invest in their success. As an investing philanthropist, you enjoy watching your donations yield results. You are willing to provide ongoing financial support, and you are willing to commit your personal time as well. If you are an investing philanthropist, you are likely to enjoy serving on a charitable board to lend your personal expertise to the organization's goals.

THE PROBLEM-SOLVING PHILANTHROPIST

Perhaps you are committed to solving some of the challenges in our world. You already know the problems that fuel your passions. As a problem-solving philanthropist, you search out organizations that address a problem that concerns you, and you use your wealth to support the efforts of one or more of these organizations. Perhaps you even help coordinate various organizations addressing your single cause so your financial and personal efforts become focused on potential solutions to specific economic, medical, or social needs.

THE SOCIAL PHILANTHROPIST

If you are in the fourth group, which I call social philanthropists, you are outgoing and passionate, and people enjoy being around you. When you choose your charitable priorities, others tend to rally around you to help accomplish your mission. Your efforts are likely to be financial and organizational. As a social philanthropist, you are energized by organizing benefits, social activities, and capital campaigns. Your efforts also often raise the public profile of your chosen causes.

Which of these categories seems to fit you best? Once you see yourself in one of these roles, you can begin to build a strategic, clutter-free approach to your philanthropy.

FOUR STEPS TO CLUTTER-FREE PHILANTHROPY

1. Articulate your mission.
2. Develop a decision making process.
3. Review your estate and financial documents.
4. Determine the appropriate charitable vehicles.

ARTICULATE YOUR MISSION

Once you have decided which strategic approach to charity describes you best, start considering how you might define your philanthropic mission. Do you have guiding principles that shape those values that you would like your family to share? Do you have tangible outcomes that you would like to achieve?

Make a list of the two or three most important values you would like reflected in your philanthropic strategy. Now list one or two tangible outcomes you would like to achieve. Use these items to draft a mission statement that concisely reflects your new strategic approach to philanthropy. For instance:

It is important to the Smith Family to use our wealth to better health care in our society and to improve the lives of children. We particularly value active programs that touch people in their ordinary lives. Our philanthropic mission is to provide financial support and leadership to establish local programs that can provide accessible care and reduce uninsured health care costs in our society.

The mission statement serves to help focus your efforts and avoid distractions from proposals that are outside your priorities. If you are planning to include your family in strategic philanthropy, the mission statement becomes critical for communicating your priorities to the rest of your family.

Some families eventually develop much more detailed mission statements that include the family history and legacy goals. As a start, the above process creates a simple and effective statement.

DEVELOP A DECISION MAKING PROCESS

A mission statement is quite useful to keep your efforts on track with your most important values over time. Day in and day out, however, you need to consider a process for deciding what you will support and how the other members of your family might participate in your efforts.

Even if you plan to pursue your strategic philanthropy plan without family members, you might consider some guidelines for how your efforts will be continued when you are gone. First, decide how final decisions will be reached. Would you like to initially put yourself, and then later a successor, in charge of all material decisions? Or do you prefer to eventually set up a family committee in which a majority vote will carry?

Would you like to create responsibilities and roles for other people now or in the future? Perhaps you might set up specific responsibilities for research, communication, and record keeping. Once you identify these roles, you will also need to create learning and training opportunities to support these activities. In this way, you may even attain further fulfillment and interaction with your family, or like minded people, as you all pursue a shared charitable strategy.

REVIEW YOUR ESTATE AND FINANCIAL DOCUMENTS

Next make sure you set aside a little time to be sure your estate-planning documents and your current financial documents are aligned with your new strategic approach. Eventually, you may choose to enhance your estate planning to support your charitable intent. For now, you need only verify that none of your documents are at odds with your approach.

DETERMINE THE APPROPRIATE CHARITABLE VEHICLES

With these steps you will transform your repetitive check writing into an approach that is focused, effective, and poised for fulfillment. Your last step will be to determine the ways in which you will give. You have lots of choices when you are searching for effective vehicles. In addition to funding worthy causes, these approaches offer a range of business, social, and tax benefits.

WAYS TO GIVE

As you consider how to support your charitable priorities, think of the positive impact you could make if you committed yourself to giving just 5 to 10% of your wealth to a single endeavor. Although this may seem like a large investment, a portfolio that achieves relatively modest annual growth can replenish this amount in just a few years.

A focused gift can be a tremendous boost for a charity, especially a charity that is relatively small. Small organizations often need management expertise as well as money, and your services as a board member or advisor might be highly appreciated. For a more established organization, consider funding a specific program or project in which you can get personally involved in the planning and execution. I know several families who stepped up to this level of personal participation and found the experience extremely rewarding. As a by-product, they met many like-minded donors who became valued friends and associates.

TAX BENEFITS OF CHARITABLE DONATIONS

Charitable giving also provides significant tax benefits. The current tax laws allow donors to deduct charitable cash gifts up to 50% of adjusted gross income. Appreciated securities and other tangible property are especially good vehicles for contributions because the IRS allows you to deduct the full market value of the donated security. Not only do you receive a current value deduction, but you also avoid paying capital gains tax on the amount of the appreciation. The IRS has a range of different limits on capital gain gifts that vary by qualifying charity, but generally these gifts can be deducted up to at least 20% of adjusted gross income.

These limitations shouldn't stop you from making even more significant charitable commitments because you can carry over your contributions. If you are not able to deduct the full contribution in the current year, you can deduct the excess over the next five years until it is used up. Of course, in all tax matters you should always check with your accountant as to your personal circumstances.

INTEGRATING WITH YOUR ESTATE PLAN

Charitable giving offers important estate tax benefits as well. Currently, if your estate is larger than the federal exemption allows, the U.S. Treasury will tax the excess at rates as high as 35%. In recent years, the top estate tax rate was as high as 55%. Through advance planning, however, you may be able to give this excess to charity and reduce or even eliminate future estate taxes.

Incorporating your charitable priorities into your estate plan does not have to add complexity to your initiatives. In fact, you can integrate your current endeavors into your future plans. Here are just a few of the vehicles you might choose to discuss with your charity of choice and your estate-planning attorney.

OUTRIGHT BEQUESTS

One of the simplest ways to support your philanthropic goals and to reduce your taxable estate is to identify an outright gift in your will. You can choose to distribute cash or personal property directly to any qualifying charity of your choice. The gift immediately reduces the size of your estate. Many large charitable institutions wish to know about bequests that have been written into wills, and they will often provide personal benefits to the donor throughout their lifetime as well as public recognition.

CHARITABLE REMAINDER/ CHARITABLE LEAD TRUSTS

A very common estate-planning structure for charitable priorities is the charitable remainder trust. An immediate tax-deductible gift is made to the trust. Then during your lifetime, the trust pays an annual return to an income beneficiary. You may identify yourself as the income beneficiary or someone else. Upon your death, the balance in the trust goes to the charity.

There are specific rules as to gift deductibility, payout structure, and allowable income. Generally, the payout may be calculated as a fixed rate annuity or as a variable rate payment based on the changing value of the assets. The usual range of payouts is about 5 to 8%. The goals of a charitable remainder trust are to: (1) earn enough in annual return to pay the annuity without using the original trust principal; (2) grow the principal in order to have the assets at least keep pace with inflation; and (3) provide lasting value for the charitable beneficiary at the conclusion of the trust.

Charitable lead trusts are structured similarly. With this vehicle, the charity enjoys the benefit of the annual payout during your lifetime, and the remaining assets either stay in your estate or are distributed to a different beneficiary of your choice. Here again, there are a variety of types of trust structures that are best suited to different tax goals. Your estate-planning attorney can help you choose between annuity trusts and unit trusts, and grantor trusts and non-grantor trusts depending on your personal needs.

GIFT ANNUITIES

Another charitable gift that aids in estate planning is the gift annuity. A gift annuity is not a trust but a relatively simple contract. You transfer cash, securities, or other marketable assets to the charitable organization of your choice, and the organization agrees to pay you a regular, fixed income stream for the remainder of your life. Most charities that offer gift annuities use the payout rates published by the American Council on Gift Annuities. The rates vary by your age at the time of the gift. The older you are when you enter the contract, the higher the payout rate.

Gift annuities have three common structures:

- Immediate Gift Annuities in which the donor (or annuitant) starts receiving payments immediately following the contribution.
- Deferred Payment Annuities in which the annuitant starts receiving payments at a future date chosen by the donor. A deferred annuity must start payments more than one year after the date of the contribution.
- Flexible Deferred Payment Annuities in which there is no set date for payments at the time of the contribution. Instead, the donor may choose anytime in the future to initiate payments. The longer the donor delays the annuitization, the larger the payments will be.

Gift annuities have two tax advantages. First, you receive an immediate tax deduction at the time of the gift. This is not a full charitable deduction, as you will be receiving an income stream in exchange for the permanent gift to the charity. The deduction depends on your age at the time of the gift and the amount of the income payout, but generally it is about 30 to 45% of the value of the gift. Second, the income stream can be tax advantaged. If the gift annuity is funded with cash, part of the annuity payments will be taxed as ordinary income and part will be tax-free. If the gift is funded with appreciated securities, part of the income will be taxed as ordinary income, part as capital gain, and part may be tax-free.

A gift annuity can be an attractive way to fund your charitable priorities while reducing your estate, creating a tax deduction, and enhancing your income stream. State insurance laws regulate gift annuity programs, and your payments are only guaranteed to the extent of the organization's financial strength.

PRIVATE FAMILY FOUNDATIONS

If you've decided that your estate plan can benefit from large charitable gifts and you would like a lasting legacy, you might consider establishing a private family foundation. A family foundation can identify your family name with a charitable mission and unite future generations around a worthwhile endeavor. You might be surprised to learn that you don't have to be Bill and Melinda Gates to create a successful private foundation. Because you are allowed to make unlimited future donations to your foundation, an initial gift as small as $250,000 to $500,000 can get you off to a good start. To qualify with the IRS as a private charity, a family foundation must pursue a genuine charitable mission, and it must make annual gifts of about 5% of its assets.

As with other types of qualified charitable gifts, if you fund your foundation with appreciated assets, you will receive an immediate tax deduction for the full market value of appreciated property donated to your foundation, and you will avoid paying capital gains taxes on the amount of the appreciation. The important advantage of a gift to a private foundation, as compared to the other choices we have discussed, is that once you give your assets to the family foundation, you and your family can maintain full control over the wealth by making both investment and operating decisions. When the assets are wisely invested, the private foundation is likely to be sustained for many future generations to steward.

Many philanthropists particularly like family foundations because they allow children and grandchildren to participate in charitable decisions. This is an ideal way to introduce your family to financial matters and acquaint them with your philanthropic ideals, without needing to disclose the extent of your personal wealth. You can bring the younger people together with the adults to discuss family giving decisions, or you can give them practical experience by allowing them to make their own giving decisions regarding a modest amount of wealth. The foundation can also provide ongoing family activities and even employment for family members. I've encountered a number of instances in which utilizing philanthropy in this way has helped keep families together long after the parents or grandparents are gone. Instead of stressful discussions about their inherited wealth, family members come together to pursue the values you have passed on and to refine their own values about important priorities in our society.

Your success puts you in a position to have a profound effect on the world. Every person who has ever made a gift to a worthy cause understands the satisfaction that comes from helping others. With a few steps, you can take your efforts to a more effective level. With focus and vision, you can make a significant difference and perhaps support your legacy goals as well.

Closing Thoughts

Your wealth should bring security, opportunity, and independence, not needless complexity, vexing decisions, and sleepless nights. Too often financial success can lead you down many unintended paths. Stuck in a maze of questions and choices, you spend too much energy controlling your wealth and not enough exploring its benefits. This is no way to enjoy your financial success.

I hope this clutter-free approach to wealth reveals to you a clear path through the maze and onto a purposeful wealth strategy of empowerment and control.

We at Summit Place Financial Advisors, LLC, stand ready to help you in any way possible. I'd love to hear from you. Once you have benefited from your clutter-free plan for a while, please reach out and share your story with me. Your success is very fulfilling to us, and I may ask you for permission to post it on our website as an encouragement to others.

Elizabeth K. Miller, CFA & CFP®
Summit Place Financial Advisors, LLC
www.summitplacefinancial.com
908.517.5880

Appendix A: Net Worth Worksheet

DESCRIPTION	YOU	SPOUSE	JOINT	TOTAL
Cash Accounts				
Savings and Checking Accounts				
CDs				
Taxable Marketable Securities				
Investment Accounts				
Mutual Funds Accounts				
Trusts Accounts				
Options				
Restricted Stock				
Tax-Deferred Marketable Securities				
IRAs, Roth IRAs, 401(k)/403(b)/457 Accounts				
Deferred Compensation Plans				
Annuities				
Personal Property				
Residences				
Investment Real Estate				
Cash Value Life Insurance				
Collectibles, Art, Jewelry				
Business Assets				
Ownership in Business Assets				
Family Assets				
Family Trusts				
Family Limited Partnerships				
TOTAL ASSETS				
Personal Debt				
Mortgages				
Lines of Credit				
Margin Debt				
Other Long-term Debt				
Business Debt				
Personally Guaranteed Debt				
Family Debt				
Debt for Family Held Assets				
TOTAL DEBT				
Total Assets -Total Debt=Total Net Worth:				

Appendix B: Critical Records Organizer

EMERGENCY CONTACTS	
Name	**Phone/Contact Information**

SAFETY DEPOSIT BOX			
Bank Name and Address	**Box #**	**Name of Joint Tenants**	**Location of Key**

SECURE INFORMATION	
Location of User IDs and Passwords	**Date Last Updated**

PERSONAL INFORMATION	
Primary Person	
Name	
Date of Birth	
Citizenship	
SSN	
Significant Other	
Name	
Date of Birth	
Citizenship	
SSN	

CHILDREN/DEPENDENTS			
Name	Contact Information	Date of Birth	SSN

PERSONAL ADVISORS			
Role	Name/Company	Contact Information	Phone
Financial Advisor			
Attorney			
Accountant			
Primary Physician			
Insurance Representative			
Estate Executor			
Clergy			

BUSINESS/PROFESSIONAL DOCUMENTS	
Document Title	**Description/Location**
Partnership/LLC Documents	
Corporate Documents	
Inventory of Business Assets	
Buy/Sell Agreements	
Other (e.g. Deferred Compensation Agreement)	

INSURANCE POLICIES		
DESCRIPTION	NAME OF INSURED	POLICY #
Health/Medical		
Life Insurance		
Long-Term Care		
Property/Casualty		
Disability		
Automobile		

FINANCIAL ASSETS			
DESCRIPTION	ACCOUNT #	COMPANY	CONTACT
Checking/Savings Accounts			
Certificates of Deposit			
Investment Accounts			
Retirement Plans (IRAs, 401(k))			
Stock Certificates			
Stock Option Plans			
Mortgages/Leases			

PROPERTY PAPERS	
DESCRIPTION	LOCATION
Vehicle Titles	
Deeds to Real Property	
Boat Ownership Records	
Copyrights and Patents	
Important Receipts	

INFORMATION NEEDED IN CASE OF INCAPACITY	
Document	Location
Power of Attorney for Health Care	
Power of Attorney for General Affairs	
Living Will	

INFORMATION NEEDED IN CASE OF DEATH	
Document	Location/Info
Final Instructions/Funeral Instructions	
Will	
Living Trust	
Cemetery Plot Records	
Pension Info for Beneficiary/Survivor	

OTHER PERSONAL DOCUMENTS	
Document	Location/Info
Birth Certificate	
Passport	
Citizenship Papers	
Military Papers	
Marriage Certificate	
Divorce Papers	
SSN Cards	

Liz Miller brings more than 20 years' experience to Summit Place Financial Advisors, LLC with a depth of investing and analytical experience that is rare in the advising industry. Her years in security analysis, portfolio management, and investment committee leadership uniquely qualify Summit Place to offer personalized investment solutions to elite families and individuals.

Liz started her career on Wall Street as a mergers and acquisition analyst in the mid 1980s. In the 1990s, she became a portfolio manager of equity mutual funds. In addition to working through the first World Trade Center bombing attempt, she gained first-hand knowledge of the inner workings of the mutual fund industry. After deciding she wanted to work more closely with individual clients, she joined a boutique investment firm in New York City where she became a principal owner. There she managed institutional and individual investment portfolios and their client relationships. She also rose to lead the firm's equity research activities and Investment Committee stock selections.

During her fifteen year tenure with the firm, she witnessed families looking to their investment managers for increasingly varied financial answers and identified the need for an advisory firm that could help simplify the increasingly complex demands on wealth. Summit Place Financial Advisors was established to deliver a broad range of financial expertise to help successful clients re-gain control of their wealth with a goals-oriented approach previously reserved only for high-end family offices.

Liz received a B.S in economics from The Wharton School at the University of Pennsylvania and an M.A. from Columbia University. She holds the Chartered Financial Analyst designation from the CFA Institute, the Chartered Investment Counselor designation from the Investment Advisor Association, and the Certified Financial Planner® designation.

Liz is a member of the Board of Trustees for the New York Society of Security Analysts and is a past chair of the Private Wealth Management Committee there for which she was honored with a Volunteer of the Year Award. She served on the Private Wealth Advisory Committee for the CFA Institute where she and others provided global leadership in identifying the industry's priorities and setting an educational agenda for private wealth professional excellence. Liz has also served as a judge for the CFA Institute Research Challenge and NYU's Berkeley School Entrepreneurial Challenge. Liz is the current Treasurer for of the Essex Skating Club of NJ and the Buck Hill Skytop Music Festival. She is a member of the Women's Presidents Organization and each summer, she joins the faculty of the Chautauqua Institute's Special Studies program leading programs in wealth management.

Liz Miller is also a regular guest in the financial media including print, radio and TV. She has been a guest on CNBC, Reuters, BNN, and Businessweek TV. She has been quoted in The Wall Street Journal and Reuters news wires, and she may be heard on Wall Street Journal radio and Dow Jones' Marketwatch. She serves on the editorial advisory board for Trusts and Estates Magazine.

Liz lives in Summit, New Jersey with her husband and twin daughters.